HAVE A BLEEDIN GUESS

The Story of Hex Enduction Hour

Paul Hanley

Published by Route
PO Box 167, Pontefract, WF8 4WW
info@route-online.com
www.route-online.com

First Paperback Edition 2020

ISBN: 978-1-901927-80-1

Paul Hanley asserts his moral
right to be identified as the author of this work

Cover design:
Golden

Printed in EU by Pulsio SARL

CONTENTS

PART III: – W/M.S. – BIG PERSONALITY FACE

For Roseanna, Adam and Nathan,
who know all about harmony

(1hr)   (1hr)   (1hr)

HEX ENDUCTION HOUR
BY THE FALL

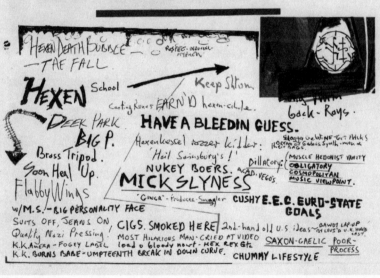

THE WHOLE EARTH SHUDDERS!
HEX ENDUCTION HOUR UNMASKED!

In 2002, nearly two decades ago now, I was invited to pitch a proposal for one of the initial half-dozen of the new 33 1/3rd publisher's studies of classic albums. I asked if I could write on the record that remains, unquestionably, my favourite of all time, The Fall's *Hex Enduction Hour*, but my suggestion was rejected as 'too uncommercial'.

How could they have resisted the mighty *Hex*? I believe it was I who wrote, in April 2019, 'The Fall's fourth album, released in 1982, saw a telepathically tight band, for many the finest frontman Mark E. Smith ever marshalled, mangle the pre-punk outsiders they loved – Can, The Velvets, Beefheart and The Stooges – into a sound unlike any rock music that preceded it. Two drum kits drove the cheesewire guitars of Craig Scanlon and Marc Riley. Steve Hanley's inch-thick electricity cable basslines simultaneously shaped the songs and shook their foundations. And unlike other singers, Mark E. Smith did not promise to mend my broken heart. *Hex* offered only an incomprehensible alienation and anger that nascent adolescence recognised. I responded to *Hex* on a primal level. It bypassed sense, understanding, and conditioning. It still does.'

33 1/3rd's debutante line-up subsequently emerged, a *Hex*-free list of *Mojo*-orthodoxies; Dusty Springfield's *Dusty In Memphis*, Love's *Forever Changes*, Neil Young's *Harvest*, Pink Floyd's *Piper At The Gates Of Dawn*, and The Smiths' *Meat Is Murder*, alongside the then still forgotten *The Kinks Are The Village Green Preservation Society*, a record from which grumpy enemies of nostalgia could conceivably take some *Hex*-flavoured comforts.

Today, 140 books down the line, *Hex Enduction Hour* is still markedly absent from the 33 1/3rd canon (the self-confessed Hexen-schooled Pavement made the grade), though in April 2019 the record deservedly earned a place in Q magazine's countdown of the '156 Most Influential Records Of All Time', and I was invited to plead its case to the organ's readers.

In retrospect, I'm delighted that I never got to write my *Hex Enduction Hour* book, because now we have Paul Hanley's instead; and it's impossible to think of anyone better to have delivered this landmark, and yet deeply personal, analysis of this landmark, and yet deeply problematic, record.

I, a smitten fan who was a psychologically vulnerable thirteen-year-old photocopy of a person when *Hex* came out, would have gushed my way through a scattershot analysis, riven by an unacknowledged oedipal struggle with the singer, and soiled by the inescapable sense disciples of great records have that the album was in some way written for their benefit, to talk directly to them, to save their insignificant selves. *Hex Enduction Hour* changed my life!! Without it the world would never have felt the benefit of my magnificent thoughts!!! Get over y'self!!!!

Twenty years ago, I went to Reykjavik, to drink in The Café Iol, as mentioned in the wyrd-folk jam 'Iceland', and I saw some 'pipes of aluminium' in the Cathedral, and maybe, I suspected, even the entrance to 'the underpants show'; and many a Winter's evening have I stood, in dazed wonder, on my way from the railway station and the comedy club, in front of the former Regal Cinema, Hitchin, where the bulk of *Hex Enduction Hour* was recorded, awaiting some kind of holy revelation in the Hertfordshire half-light. My *Hex* book would, inevitably, have been all about me, and my heroic efforts to decode the great work. And it would have been shit.

Thank God we have instead the definitive *Hex* study, written by a man who played on it, lived through it, and who has now amassed both the critical tools, and the critical distance, required to appraise it accurately. Former Fall drummer Paul Hanley joins his brother, former Fall bassist Steve Hanley, as a late blooming literary talent, now able to make the case for *Hex*'s greatness without either the rose-tinted Ray-Bans or the self-righteous rancour that often characterises such revisionist efforts.

Paul has pulled off something of a literary sleight of hand here, balancing the demands of fact-frenzied fans, with the desire to produce a narrative of substance and style. Yes, he offers us the meticulous cataloguing of recording dates of individual songs, locations of sessions, and precise details of equipment where available. But Paul also charts his own path, as a teenager thrown into the deep end on the drum stool of a resolutely non-rock rock band, and tells us tales even obsessives have never heard before. Who knew, for example, that 'Mere Pseud Mag. Ed.' owes a musical debt to 'Baby Sitters', the one-off 1979 single by the eleven-year-old Adamski's infant-punk duo Stupid Babies? I didn't know that. And I know everything.

And just as God is in the details, so Paul Hanley is in the footnotes. For me, the footnote is a massively underrated literary device, and it is my aim to one day produce a book which is mainly comprised of footnotes at the expense of the main narrative itself. Paul is a modern master of the footnote, and switches tone from a more detached and objective mode in the text proper, to a gossipy and sometimes indiscreet mode below the line, letting slip with good-humoured indulgence the sort of dynamite trivia fans love, satiating our needy hunger and our pathetic longing.

In the main text, Paul is reading aloud at a lectern at a book festival in a severe-looking publicly-funded building. In the footnotes, you've cornered him afterwards, in the Wetherspoon's across the road, and he's spilling his secrets all over one of Tim Martin's bespoke regional carpet designs.

Above all, one takes away from *Have A Bleedin Guess* the sense that Paul Hanley is, to quote the catchphrase of Robert Lloyd of the Nightingales (who, we learn, sold Marc Riley a guitar with a strap signed by Link Wray) a 'good bloke'. Musicians' memoirs can tend to fixate on the settling of scores, the avoidance of blame, and the righting of imagined wrongs. The Fall's figurehead Mark E. Smith left chaos and anger in his wake, but though Paul sets a few facts about songwriting credits straight, the Hexen hour is long enough ago now for him to weigh equally and fairly the strengths and weaknesses of the tense personal dynamics that made that classic Fall line-up function as it did. In short, there's a generosity of spirit in *Have A Bleedin Guess* that is often absent from rock musicians' recollections of their time in the field.

In moments of doubt, when my faith is tested by the easy emotional comforts of Alt Country troubadours or the sugar rush thrills of vintage psychedelia, I wonder if I would still think *Hex Enduction Hour* was the greatest rock album of all time if I had been old enough to stumble across the sounds and scribes that informed it – all those weird '70s Germans, pre-punk New York pioneers, and syntax-bending Vorticists – before it got a hold of my soul.

Get behind me Satan! Paul Hanley's meticulous and charming *Have A Bleeding Guess* washes all my doubts away and I am born again. Of course *Hex Enduction Hour* is the greatest rock album of all time. Whatever was I thinking?

Stewart Lee
Writer/Clown
Buxa/Stoke Newington
August/September 2019

HEX REX Etc

I'm still very proud of that album. It's the one everybody talks about, and I can see why.

Mark E. Smith, 2009

There's always some cunt who wants to ask me about a masterpiece I made in 1982.

Mark E. Smith, 2015

Why *would* you want to talk about an album you made 37 years ago? Well, even Mark E. Smith could see why *Hex Enduction Hour*, The Fall's fourth LP,[1] remained one of their most critically lauded and fondly-remembered. If you've read either *Renegade* or *The Big Midweek,* you'll also know that the story of The Fall is an interesting one in itself. If you're a fan of the group[2] who'd like to know more about the way the group worked, then the period when *Hex Enduction Hour* was created is a good place to start.

John Doran: Even if it's a fool's errand trying to decide which is the greatest LP out of The Fall's huge back catalogue of albums, many fanatics of the group will tell you that the worst thing you can say about *Hex* is that it's their equal best at the very least.

Given that it was issued in the heyday of vinyl, most labels presented with sixty minutes of music would have chosen to release it as a double album. After all, *Exile on Main St.* is only seven minutes longer, and *London Calling* would be pretty much the same length as *Hex* but for the last-minute, unlisted addition of 'Train in Vain'. In fact, *Hex* would have been longer than both if 'And This Day' hadn't been pruned down to a more manageable

---

[1] Or fifth if you count *Slates.*
[2] I suspect you might be.

length (10:23!) so the album would fit its title. In some ways it's a shame *Hex Enduction Hour* isn't a double – it's certainly capable of shouldering the extra gravitas such a designation customarily infers. Of course, it's likely a desire to avoid such jaded preconceptions is precisely what made Mark E. Smith insist that the songs were crammed onto two sides of a single album.

Because of the way The Fall worked in those days, *Hex* and its contents can't be discussed in a vacuum. Even though Fall records were released with alarming regularity in the early eighties, recorded output was still unable to keep pace with the band's prolific songwriting. Though 1982 saw the group release some twenty new tracks, many of them, including most of *Hex Enduction Hour,* had vanished from the set by the time we toured Australia and New Zealand in July and August that year.

If we count from when Karl Burns returned to the group, which we probably should, then the line-up that recorded *Hex* lasted from May 1981's European tour, when Karl and I played on alternate nights, until December 1982, when Marc Riley was dismissed. In that 19-month period, the group played around 130 gigs: there were four trips round the UK, tours of the Netherlands, West Germany, Belgium, the USA, Australia, New Zealand and Iceland, and even a brief excursion to Greece. The Fall released three singles, two of which weren't on an LP, and two albums. There was also the customary session for John Peel and two contemporaneously released live albums which are still in circulation today. Clearly, for the seven people that comprised the group at that time (the six band members and Kay Carroll, our manager) The Fall was pretty much all we did. *Hex Enduction Hour* was just a part of it.

None of which is to imply it isn't a coherent and discrete piece of work. Though two of its tracks were recorded in Iceland before Karl was officially installed as a second drummer, most of it was recorded over a two-week period in Hitchin, Hertfordshire, and has a palpably homogenous feel. Mark was determined to present his new label Kamera with a product that would sell well and thereby put two fingers up to his old label, Rough Trade.

If the circumstance of its recording afforded it a more singular vision than its predecessor, *Grotesque,* then it definitely fostered a degree of finesse that its follow-up, *Room To Live,* couldn't hope to emulate.

While what went on during the Iceland and Hitchin sessions will inform much of what follows, documenting the making of *Hex Enduction Hour* isn't like discussing *Rumours,* or even *Blood on the Tracks:* its recording was part of a process. What's more, the Fall process often subverted the rehearse-record-tour cycle by skipping the rehearsal bit – it wasn't unheard of for a song roughed out in a soundcheck to be part of that night's set. The oldest song on *Hex Enduction Hour* was first played live as early as August 1980. The group released an LP, a six-track 'mini-album' and two singles before it made its way onto vinyl, but it fits *Hex Enduction Hour*'s atmosphere perfectly. Someone in The Fall knew what they were doing. Hopefully by the end of this you'll have some idea too.

While it would be remiss of anyone endeavouring to tell the story of an album to not attempt at least some discussion of its lyrical content, deciphering a song's words inevitably involves more theorising and/or guesswork than the other aspects of the story. Moreover, in some instances, discussions about 'authorial intent' become all but meaningless anyway – Mark has declared on occasion that he wasn't aware what his intentions *were* when writing a particular lyric.

Mark E. Smith: I always try and put a little crack in it, and I always try and put lyrics that mean nothing and like jumble it all up [...] Lyrics change shape and meaning all the time [...] and do you know, I don't always have a fucking clue what I'm saying. They can be just off my head. I don't mean I'm off my head. I mean the words just come off the top of my head. It's a bastard because when we have to do it live it means I have to sit down and listen to them and play it again and again. But some of my best songs are like that. A quarter of it is done on the spot. If you write everything down it's chaos.

So, 'Have a bleedin guess', along with 'What's it mean? What's it mean?' from 'New Puritan', should be viewed as Mark E. Smith's default retort to those who would attempt to decode and thus demystify his lyrics. As with many artists (as in 'people who make art' rather than 'recording artists'), attempts to limit the meaning of Mark's works to what he was thinking when he created them risk diminishing those works immeasurably. Or as he himself put it:

Mark E. Smith: When I started buying records, the ones I liked were the ones I could only half-understand. What I don't like about a lot of records today is that they're too clear. There's no fascination or mystery left. [...] This culture where you have to explain everything all the time, what you're doing, puts a clamp on you. It's a bit of a trap.

So, does 'The Classical' mean what he meant when he first wrote it? Or what he believed when he sang it onstage four months later? The flip side of such diversions into 'new criticism' is the worry that Mark's lyrics, and thus Mark himself, are afforded higher status by dint of one reading more into them than is actually there – 'The Emperor's New Clothes' by way of *Being There*. And Mark was often his own worst enemy in allowing that belief to propagate, as renowned Manchester music journalist Paul Morley has admitted:

Paul Morley: What if he wasn't a genius, he was just an old drunken tramp that when he got really drunk started to spout phrases that made a kind of sense and we read too much into it?

It's a good quote, and it's something that has crossed many people's minds at one time or another, but it's obviously not true, as Morley knew when he said it. When he could be bothered, Mark had both the erudition and self-taught literary expertise to disprove this theory in an instant. There were periods of his life when he probably didn't do that often enough, but his disinclination to justify himself is one of the main differences between The Fall and every other group. He really didn't care whether you got it, it was your loss.

In short, any interesting theories about the words, whether my own or advanced elsewhere and quoted here, are just that. And the one thing we can be sure of is that Mark would dismiss them at a stroke.[3]

Another difference between The Fall and other acts of similar vintage or older was that Mark E. Smith steadfastly refused to make The Fall's history part of the act. He was so stubbornly uninterested in looking back that it alienated a section of his potential audience, which in turn had a direct impact on his earnings. Whether that made them a better live prospect depends, I suppose, on your attitude to nostalgia. Personally, I've always been delighted when Buzzcocks played 'Boredom' (or 'Nostalgia' for that matter), when Lydon sings 'Public Image' or when Johnny Marr strums the opening chords to 'How Soon Is Now?'. It's not, of course, what I expected of The Fall. Because for Mark E. Smith, The Fall was always about *now*.

Stewart Lee: Compared to The Fall, even Dylan's apparently sacrilegious approach to the casual rephrasing of his own legacy of song seems accommodating and respectful. … Smith refuses to become a keeper of sacred relics.

Re-evaluating his group's prodigious back catalogue was never a priority for Mark E. Smith. That doesn't mean that I, or anyone else, should have felt the same. Trying to follow Mark's lead when deciding which Fall product should be held in the highest regard was always as pointless as it was impossible,[4] not least because he was an inveterate revisionist, and often wilfully contradictory from one pronouncement to the next, as illustrated

---

[3] The relationship between author and those who expect him to dissect his work for their benefit is brilliantly (and hilariously) explored in Mark's lyric to 'How I Wrote Elastic Man'. He doesn't even say 'Elastic'.

[4] You'll know this if you've ever spent more than two minutes looking at the discussion board of TheFall.org.

by the two quotes above. This reached its hilarious zenith in 2009 when he was often to be found disputing both facts and opinions as reported *in his own autobiography*. Besides, any work of art transcends its author's intentions the moment it enters the public domain. There is also the obvious point (to some at least) that he wasn't the author of *Hex Enduction Hour*, he was a co-author. There were six people involved in the writing, and seven in the performance, of the material that constitutes *Hex*, and no one was reading sheet music. I know this because I was there.[5]

Perhaps the overriding, and certainly the saddest, reason why now is a good time to re-evaluate *Hex Enduction Hour* is that the difference between current Fall fans and those Mark liked to call 'look back bores' has been eradicated by his death. The idea that harking back to a bygone era is somehow disrespectful to the current incarnation of The Fall has finally gone forever: it's all the old stuff now.

[5] As will quickly become apparent, this can add a degree of double-think to the writing. Try not to get seasick as the narrative, by necessity, veers between 'they' and 'we'. And, much more importantly, remember that I loved The Fall both before and after I was a member, so if I say certain things are great, it's never because I'm on them.

PART I
OBLIGATORY COSMOPOLITAN MUSIC VIEWPOINT

SAXON – GAELIC

The first Fall line-up to release records was famously a more democratic unit than subsequent line-ups, which is probably the reason it was destined not to last. Original keyboard player Una Baines and bassist Tony Friel only appeared on one, three-track EP, *Bingo-Master's Break-Out!*, before giving way to Yvonne Pawlett and Johnny Brown/Eric McGann then Marc Riley respectively. Guitarist and main co-composer Martin Bramah and drummer Karl Burns managed another single, 'It's the New Thing', and one album, *Live at the Witch Trials,* before they jumped ship too. Karl was the first to go – his drumming was highly regarded and lauded in live reviews, so he thought it might be a good idea to capitalise on this by securing a more lucrative gig before the goodwill wore off. Graham Lock's *NME* review of *Witch Trails* nicely summed up what Karl brought to the party: 'His superb drumming holds them together, drives it along, rescues it from the possibility of formless repetition (and I wonder how they'll fire/fare now that he's gone).' *Melody Maker* on the other hand, was adamant that 'Karl Burns … is not an especially adept or versatile drummer', which is about as close to being factually incorrect as an opinion can get. To be fair, Allan Jones's attitude to every aspect of *Live at the Witch Trials* was more than a little supercilious. Mark's vocals, for instance, were dismissed as 'a cross between Howard Devoto and Eddie Waring'.

Bramah stayed on just long enough to oversee the recruitment of Karl's successor, Mike Leigh. The line-up of Smith, Bramah, Riley, Pawlett and Leigh only played a dozen gigs, and never recorded anything, not even a session for John Peel. Uncomfortable with the more autocratic direction the group was heading in,[6]

---

[6] **Martin Bramah:** It was becoming hard work with Mark and the management. It was getting a bit dictatorial and we were just 19-20-year-old kids. I wanted to be wild and free and do my own thing.

Martin told Mark of his decision to leave on 20th April 1979, at an Iggy Pop gig at the Factory in Hulme.[7] To the outside world at least, the group accepted the departure of its founder member and main songwriter with barely a shrug. The Fall were back on stage by 9th May.

In truth, once he'd got over the shock, Mark was galvanised by Martin's departure. 'The energy a line-up change injects into a band is incredible,' he told Tony Fletcher later that year – and it was clearly a lesson he never forgot. Marc Riley's friends Craig Scanlon (guitar) and Steve Hanley (bass) were hastily drafted in to cover the shortfall – there were no diary clashes to contend with as they were already on board as unpaid roadies and sometime support band Staff 9. The new Riley/Scanlon/Hanley team constituted the core of the band for the next three years, and quickly formed a powerful and prolific songwriting partnership.

Yvonne Pawlett completed her tour of duty after recording the 'Rowche Rumble' single. It was reported at the time that she left to look after her dog, but it was more a case of not fitting in. Her sense of isolation was exacerbated by the fact that the band now consisted of a couple on one side and three school friends on the other. Having to stay in Mark and Kay's spare room every time the group rehearsed or played can't have been much of a picnic either.

It's useful to think of *Dragnet* as a debut album – it was, to all intents and purposes, the first LP by the group that wrote and recorded *Hex Enduction Hour*. The only musician left from *Witch Trial*'s line-up was Marc Riley, and he'd had little involvement in that album's composition.[8]

Mark's unique lyrical stylings and acerbic delivery aside, almost everything about *Dragnet* was different from The Fall's previous album. Having an out-and-out bass player, rather than a guitarist playing bass, was one significant departure – Steve

---

[7] Pop's set that night included the Stooges' semi (if you'll pardon the pun)-obscure classic 'Cock in My Pocket' which The Fall got around to covering live a mere 35 years later, and recording, as 'Stout Man', on 2015's *Sub-Lingual Tablet*.

[8] He did receive a songwriting credit on 'Music Scene' but the band were playing it live at least a month before he joined. Previous bassist Eric McGann, aka Rick Goldstraw, aka 'Ferret', was somewhat put-out at Marc's acknowledgement.

always wrote for the bass, and the other instrumentalists had to add appropriate lines or chords on top of that – an unusual way of doing things which would inform the Fall sound for years to come.

What's more, for the time being at least, no one was playing keyboards, except as an afterthought. Instead, all the songs featured a second guitar, which made for a denser, less open sound.

There was also a radical change to the percussion: Mike Leigh's drumming was ridiculously different from Karl Burns, both in terms of the sound of his kit[9] and his technique. As coincidence would have it, Kenney Jones inherited The Who's drum stool from the late Keith Moon at almost exactly the same time as The Fall replaced Karl Burns with Mike Leigh. With hindsight, no one thinks that was a good fit, but the transition was seamless compared to the impact that swapping Karl for Mike had on the group's sound.

We're given a unique opportunity to explore this difference, and the dissimilarity between the *Witch Trials* and *Dragnet* line-ups as a whole, by comparing the version of 'Put Away' recorded for the John Peel show on the 27th November 1978 with the version recorded in August 1979 for *Dragnet*. In terms of drumming, switching to a swing beat rather than straight 4/4 is a tried and tested method of making a song feel lighter and less oppressive – so it's puzzling why Leigh thought that was an appropriate shift for a tale about a man contemplating a life in solitary confinement. This change in feel is also at odds with the other sonic developments – the loss of Pawlett's jaunty keyboards and the cloying nature of the whole album's sound. Another significant difference is that the *Dragnet* version, like much of the LP, is so clearly out of tune you could be forgiven for suspecting it

[9] Karl, like many drummers at that time, including me, preferred no bottom skin on his toms, which allows for more volume and attack but far less resonance. Mike's sparkly Premier kit was replete with a full complement of bottom heads. What's more, it boasted real goat-skin top heads which required a delicacy of touch that Karl couldn't have managed even if he'd wanted to. Mike's signing-on fee for the band also included the purchase of a set of four Rototoms – shell-less toms, developed by Remo, which resonate to the point where they have a definite pitch, unlike conventional drums. They were horrible.

must be deliberate.[10] The guitar part, which is the core of the song, is mostly the same in both versions, apart from Craig's use of slide guitar on the second solo. In fact the song is far more indebted to Martin Bramah than the credits ('Smith') would perhaps suggest.

By far the most discomfiting change between debut and sophomore albums is the production. Both are recordings of five people playing live in the same room, and neither album was subjected to much in the way of overdubs or studio jiggery-pokery, but they both have an identifiable 'sound' which is nothing like the other's. *Dragnet*'s sonic palette was, for the most part, a sombre one. Recorded at Rochdale's 16-track Cargo Studios, it was produced by Grant Showbiz, who would be an integral part of the Fall story from *Dragnet* right up to 2013's *Re-Mit*.

As a schoolboy Grant Cunliffe had followed legendary hippy outfit Gong up and down the country and eventually ended up working and living with their guitarist Steve Hillage.

Grant Showbiz: At fifteen, dear old Gong invited me back to their farm in Oxford and suddenly I was initiated into the whole running of a band – Steve Hillage took me under his wing when I was seventeen and taught me basic sound control skills. My first professional gig was guitar roadie for Steve when he supported Queen in Hyde Park. That was where I saw my first proper mixing desk – love at first sight.

When Hillage's new band, 'L', decamped to the USA, Cunliffe began working with another off-shoot of Gong: Here & Now, who christened him 'Showbiz' due to his ostentatious possession of a briefcase. As the decade wore on, Showbiz became increasingly interested in the new music that was appearing in London's clubs, though he quickly became disillusioned with punk's first wave.

---

[10] Scottish band The Fire Engines certainly believed it – they later admitted copying this 'technique' of having one guitar slightly off-pitch on their earliest singles. Not that Mark was flattered by the imitation. In 1982 he commented, 'Like you get all these Scottish bands in England, they do 15-20 minutes and they're not even in tune at the end of the fucking set.' In any case, the fact that The Fall stopped sounding like that immediately after Will Sergeant from Echo & The Bunnymen introduced them to the electronic guitar tuner is probably all you need to know.

Grant Showbiz: I'd seen Alternative TV at the 100 Club in the spring of 1978, and I realised that something was afoot – away from the twelve-bar Pistols and Damned effect.

Showbiz asked Mark Perry what other bands he'd recommend.[11]

Grant Showbiz: Mark P played me *Bingo* and my life changed forever. The first Fall gig I saw was at The Greyhound, supporting Siouxsie and the Banshees. I had an immediate rapport with Mark and Kay, so I offered them the chance of doing support gigs with Here & Now. We had a PA, and we organised free tours of all the major towns in the UK.

Anticipating the couple's understandable wariness about doing gigs for free, Showbiz pointed out that this would be exposure that The Fall hadn't had up till then. He also agreed to do their live sound, which was a major step forward for the group. Before Grant, they'd been forced to work with whatever person came with the PA.

Grant Showbiz: Generally club owners and PA guys hated the Fall sound, whereas to me it was a thing of intricate beauty. I became a sympathetic ear who understood how they should sound, something Mark hadn't found before outside Manchester.

Showbiz's absolute confidence that he knew how to present the group made him a natural choice for the role of *Dragnet*'s producer. By the time he'd finished, its production was as far from the prevailing wisdom as the Joy Division and Public Image Limited albums which were released the same year. But while posterity has labelled *Unknown Pleasures* and *Metal Box* as harbingers of a new and much imitated soundscape, *Dragnet*'s sound remains unapologetically unique, as Showbiz is happy to testify.

[11] Perry was the singer with Alternative TV. If you haven't heard their brilliant debut album *The Image Has Cracked* I'd advise you to do so post-haste. He was also the figurehead for Step Forward Records (though Miles Copeland was the money), who'd released the *Bingo-Master's Break-Out!* EP.

Grant Showbiz: We went into Rochdale with a shared vision, which involved throwing out all ideas other than our own. The engineer sat at the back of the room listening to ABBA on his Walkman while we did exactly as we liked, including all the mic placements. Afterwards I realised that the house engineer would normally help out, but I insisted he didn't touch the desk. What I learned was enormous – to trust a band, let them do what they do best and capture it. Brilliant inspired writing and playing makes a record more than production tricks. What a band sound like in the studio is not what they will eventually sound like coming through a home stereo – so that has to be taken into consideration when mixing. More than anything you need to be aware that 'studio' and 'live' are two different situations which need different methods of work.

John Brierley, who ran Cargo, remembers the session slightly differently.

John Brierley: I was always proud of *Dragnet* and all the Fall tracks I engineered and co-produced. The unusual sonic sound was unique to Cargo and one of the reasons The Fall recorded there.

But whatever the extent of the engineer's involvement, Grant's insistence on a near-total absence of reverb and compression was the main reason why *Dragnet* sounds so damned different to everything else. Although Mark's habit of recording the vocals live in the same room as the rest of the group also had some unexpected, and literal, repercussions.

Grant Showbiz: I love the way it sounds – bar the overloud cymbal crashes caused by Mark drifting over to the drum kit at inappropriate times.

Marc Riley: The sound on *Dragnet* either freaked people out completely or it blew their minds, which I think is what Mark wanted. A song like 'A Figure Walks', produced differently, could have been massive. Which isn't to say it would necessarily have been better. There are more people out there who love *Dragnet* than *Witch Trials* because *Dragnet* is where Mark established this fragile off-kilter band of non-musicians, where Karl and Martin were brilliant musicians.

The dramatic alteration in set up and personnel between *Live at the Witch Trials* and *Dragnet* wasn't repeated for the next album. The only change was behind the kit. Mike Leigh tendered his resignation in March 1980, fully expecting to see out his notice. He was particularly keen to complete the current tour supporting The Cramps,[12] as it was due to end at Camden's Electric Ballroom, a much larger venue than he was used to. Kay, who viewed his ducking out as something of a betrayal, would have none of it. She declared she'd rather do the prestigious gig with an untested, unrehearsed 16-year-old than give Mike the opportunity to bow out gracefully,[13] and I was hastily brought on board, initially just to fulfil the commitment of the final date on 21st March. Because of The Fall's rapid turnover in material, five of the songs the group played that night were unrecorded.[14] This turned out to be a blessing in many ways, as it meant I had no idea what Mike had done with them. None of the band was sufficiently proficient in musical theory to articulate what they'd heard, even if they'd been listening to him, which is doubtful. So I was pretty much left to my own devices. As there was no time for a full band

---

[12] The Cramps were a brilliant bass-less pyschobilly group and an original part of the CBGB's punk scene. Sadly, of the classic line-up that toured with The Fall, only guitarist 'Poison' Ivy Rorschach is still with us. Singer Lux Interior, guitarist Bryan Gregory and drummer Nick Knox have all gone for a date with Elvis.

[13] It's hard to reconcile Leigh's given reason for departure – lack of gigs – with the group's schedule. Between joining in February 1979, and leaving in March 1980, Leigh played some 90 gigs with The Fall, including an American tour. They didn't even observe the traditional long post-Christmas layoff. The final date of their US tour was 14th December, and by 10th January 1980 they were back playing Manchester Polytechnic.

[14] 'C'n'C', 'How I Wrote Elastic Man', 'City Hobgoblins', 'English Scheme' and 'Impression of J. Temperance'. I did receive some tuition on that one – the drum pattern's nicked from Gioachino Rossini's *William Tell Overture*, or more correctly the theme from *The Lone Ranger*.

rehearsal before the gig, and obviously no YouTube footage to use as homework, this meant the first time I heard the songs with vocals was live on stage.

Once I'd been fully installed as official drummer, the group resumed the loose routine of being more or less constantly on tour with the odd songwriting session and rehearsal fitted around the gigs. New songs were added in rapid succession – by the time The Fall played the Beach Club in Manchester on 28th May, a mere two months after I'd joined, nine of the fourteen songs featured in the set were unreleased. Unsurprisingly, this meant the gig had no room for anything from *Live at the Witch Trials* or its attendant single.

This laissez-faire attitude to composing new songs was crucial to the group's productiveness throughout its existence. The custom of only playing songs an audience has had a chance to hear never took hold with The Fall. It's an understandable strategy, and certainly what many audiences want, but in practice it often allows the composer to put off writing new material until absolutely necessary, i.e. when a recording session is looming. This, in turn, is a common reason for the 'difficult second album', when groups that have had their whole lives to write their first album are expected to come up with another set of songs in a matter of weeks and fail miserably. The Fall never fell victim to this because they added songs to their live set whenever they were written, with no thought given as to when, or even if, they'd be recorded.

In fact, The Fall wrote enough songs to warrant three separate recording sessions at Rochdale's Cargo Studios between May and August 1980. Following the release of the single 'Fiery Jack', its producer, Geoff Travis, had lured the group to Rough Trade, so the recordings were bankrolled by the new label. The first of the three sessions resulted in the single 'How I Wrote Elastic Man'/'City Hobgoblins', and the second yielded 'Totally Wired' and 'Putta Block'. At the third session we recorded the bulk of The Fall's third studio album, *Grotesque*.

One regular song from the set that wasn't recorded during

the *Grotesque* sessions was 'Jawbone and the Air-Rifle'. Mark obviously had plans for it, as it was later to become the oldest song on *Hex Enduction Hour*. It was written during the summer of 1980, and like everything else it was played on stage almost straightaway. The song *was* recorded for the *John Peel Show* in September, alongside 'New Puritan', a bedroom recording of which had previously been released on the mainly live album *Totale's Turns (It's Now or Never)*. The session was completed by two tracks from *Grotesque,* which had been recorded but wouldn't be released until November.

The songwriting team was broadly the same for *Dragnet* and *Grotesque,* the only difference being that by *Grotesque* they had exorcised the spectre of Martin Bramah, whose influence on *Dragnet* has always been underestimated. But the change in atmosphere between the two albums is remarkable. It was neatly reflected in the switch from black and white to full colour on their covers. As well as flagging up its content's more vibrant qualities, the cover of *Grotesque,* which was painted by Mark's sister Suzanne based on his original drawing, was designed to send a soon-to-be familiar message to those bemoaning the departure of the group's original members: 'If it's me with a spotty kid behind me, it's a Fall gig.'[15] That's always been Mark's ideal band: young, slightly in awe of him, eager to please, and grateful for the opportunity. Of course, human nature being what it is, eagerness and gratitude are almost as impossible to sustain as youth. It's probably this more than anything else that explains the periodic re-jigging of the band's membership.[16]

The best Fall iterations managed to strike a balance between realising Mark E. Smith's vision, which made them different and worth a listen; and doing exactly what he said, which had the potential to make them all-but unlistenable. And to their credit, the Riley, Scanlon and Hanley line-up were able to maintain this

---

[15] A paraphrasing of Mark's oft-repeated 'If it's me and yer granny on bongos, then it's a Fall gig'. Ninety-nine times out of a hundred this is misquoted as 'it's The Fall', which is subtlety different, if no less contemptuous of both his band and his audience.

[16] The exception that proved the rule, the group's final iteration of Pete Greenway, Dave Spurr and Keiron Melling managed to sustain this dynamic for more than 10 years, which probably makes them The Fall's most successful line-up, and certainly Mark's favourite.

delicate balance on a significant body of work, regardless of who was behind the kit.

Another change between *Dragnet* and *Grotesque* was the production. Geoff Travis had co-produced 'Elastic Man' with Mayo Thompson, guitarist in fellow Rough Trade signing Pere Ubu, but for the next single, 'Totally Wired', and *Grotesque*, Mark decided that Travis alone would be easier to bend to his will.

Geoff Travis: [Mark] asked me if he could 'not have that Mayo Thompson come this time', and like a true friend I abandoned Mayo immediately ... I not only produced *Grotesque*, I engineered it as well: me, a man who can hardly turn a stereo on. But then I think a gnat or a mosquito could produce a Fall record if it was lucky enough to be in the vicinity.

Grotesque (After the Gramme) contained at least three songs which could justifiably be described as classic Fall, not least in the way that attempts to clearly define them risk missing the point. Mark once admitted 'I don't really write from a solid idea' with specific reference to this album. Though the songs 'New Face in Hell' and 'The N.W.R.A.' all but abandoned metre and rhyme in order to tell linear stories with a beginning, a middle and an end, they're still not the easiest stories to follow. 'The N.W.R.A.' begins as a straightforward tale of Mark E. Smith's experiences during a North/South civil war as narrated by one Joe Totale.[17] However, it breaks free of the shackles of narrative cohesion before it's even halfway through. As the late author and cultural theorist Mark Fisher put it: 'The form of "The N.W.R.A." is as alien to organic wholeness as is Totale's abominable tentacular body. It is a grotesque concoction, a collage of pieces that do not belong together.' Fisher also rightly pointed out that the song 'plays like some improbable mulching of T.S. Eliot, Wyndham

[17] Roman Totale XVII, the bastard offspring of Charles I and the Great God Pan, and his yet-unborn son, Joe, acted as Mark's spokespersons and conduits on a number of records and press releases during this period. The first Fall live album was named in their honour. That album's sleeve notes reveal R. Totale was no Tony Barrow-style sycophant: 'I don't particularly like the person singing on this LP. That said, I marvel at his guts.'

Lewis, H.G. Wells, P.K. Dick, Lovecraft and Le Carré'.[18] It is about as succinct a summation of Mark's writing style as you're likely to get.

By contrast, 'New Face in Hell' has a remarkably economical word count, and the events recounted therein would play out in real time in about five minutes. The wireless enthusiast hears an illicit broadcast, nips next door, spots his friend's body and gets arrested. Roll titles. But the fact that the government agent poisons the neighbour and frames the wireless enthusiast rather than simply killing *him* opens up a host of narrative possibilities, none of which Mark sees any need to explore – which inevitably forces listeners to fill in the rest of the story's detail for themselves.

Mark was clearly fascinated by the idea of a song as an impersonal third-person narrative which revealed nothing of himself. He only succeeded in 'New Face in Hell' by stripping the narrative back to the bare minimum, and signally failed in 'The N.W.R.A.'s more expansive lyric. He would explore the idea more successfully in *Hex Enduction Hour*'s 'Jawbone and the Air-Rifle'.

The other song from *Grotesque* that could justifiably be described as classic Fall is 'The Container Drivers'. Like the earlier single 'Fiery Jack', it employed the new band's unique 'Country and Northern' template.[19] This musical style, which Mark would return to many times, was completely absent from the arsenal of the *Live at the Witch Trials* line-up. While this could lead one to conclude that it was introduced by Steve and Craig, there were no such diversions into Americana in Staff 9's set either – it was actually Marc Riley's ascent to songwriter status which added the new element. It's likely Mark welcomed this addition of country and western to the group's sound for the same reason John

---

[18] This quote is taken verbatim, and it's interesting, if a bit of a digression, to note that some of the authors are afforded their initials and some aren't. While it could be argued that the addition of 'T.S.' clarifies that Fisher doesn't mean George Eliot (given that *Middlemarch* has been cited as the source of the title of 'Middle Mass' this isn't as impossible as it sounds), but H.G. Wells? Who else could he mean – Orson? And how many 'Dick's were writing fiction in the mid-twentieth century? Answers on a postcard.
[19] 'The Container Drivers' could have also been described as following a 12-bar blues structure had anyone in the band been able to consistently count to twelve.

Lydon flirted with disco on PiL's *Metal Box*: assimilating a deeply unfashionable musical genre, which he genuinely enjoyed, in order to unsettle, shake up, and hopefully educate the more closed-eared followers of his previous band.[20] Mark would make subverting what people expected – from rock music in general as much as from The Fall – an absolutely central tenet of *Hex Enduction Hour*.

The move into less easily defined territory continued on the group's six-track 'mini-LP' *Slates*, which defied categorisation even in its physical appearance. Released on ten-inch vinyl, *Slates* was neither a single nor an LP and was thus rendered ineligible for inclusion in the indie charts, Rough Trade's main method of self-aggrandisement. Mark also sought to wrong-foot those who thought the group incapable of anything but lo-fi recording. As well as marshalling the producers of the last two albums, Grant Showbiz and Geoff Travis, to provide a best-of-both-worlds production tag-team, Mark added no less a light than Adrian Sherwood, an experienced dub producer who had previously worked with Prince Far-I, a personal favourite of Mark's.

Grant Showbiz: *Slates* was pretty much my album production-wise. I can remember Geoff Travis hanging about in the studio and being encouraging and Adrian Sherwood sending the snare sound down to a speaker in the toilet and mixing that up to get a drum sound which was pretty revolutionary stuff for me at the time. Things like basic sounds, use of acoustic guitars, double vocals, suggesting which take was best and mixing were done by me.

Adrian Sherwood: I ended up helping Grant Showbiz because he was the producer. Mark was not using any reverb, any delay, any production techniques, because he wanted to sound a certain way. So literally with ['Middle Mass'] all I did was help balance

---

[20] In our post-modern age it's difficult to appreciate just how partisan music audiences were in the late seventies/early eighties. But the 'Disco Sucks' movement, a sometimes violent backlash against dance music by rock fans in the US, was all too real. See also *Going to Sea in a Sieve* for Danny Baker's recollection of half-witted punks cheering the news of the death of Elvis Presley at the Vortex.

it. It was part of my history because I was there when *Slates* was being cut and I was there at the recording. But that's Grant Showbiz's tune. What I learnt from Mark Smith and why that record is so important, is like 'anti-production' techniques. So I got a lot off him.

Slates was another milestone on Mark's journey towards getting The Fall's records to sound like the sounds in his head. Replacing the original band with younger, more compliant musicians was a large part of this, but moulding producers to his way of thinking was also paying dividends.

Geoff Travis: Mayo came back on board for the wonderful six-track *Slates*, which Adrian Sherwood also did some good work on. It was a phenomenal record. After that, I think my days as a glorious producer were over.

Having deliberately released *Dragnet* with a production that even its staunchest supporters knew was little more than slightly-manicured noise, Mark was canny enough to ensure that its 'anti-production' didn't become the group's default setting. He gradually allowed a modicum of technique to be introduced to the point that *Slates* was even talked about in hushed tones as 'well produced'. But of course, he had no intention of sticking with that approach either. The next album, which he was already thinking of as the group's ultimate achievement, would combine the two approaches and finally unleash the sound he'd wanted all along: well-produced noise.

Mark E. Smith: What I'm going for is a well-produced noise thing. Not like bringing up the obvious things, but bringing out everything, bringing out the distortion and producing it well.

But any story about The Fall can't be told purely in terms of recording sessions. Between the release of *Grotesque* in November 1980 and *Slates* in April 1981, the group played an impressive run of British dates. As well as most of the *Slates* tracks, the 1980 concerts saw regular performances of 'Jawbone and the Air-Rifle'. The gig at London's Acklam Hall on 11th December was recorded and released in 1982 as *The Fall Live in London*.[21] The delay in its release made it seem like a conventional live album, i.e. a run through the group's back catalogue. At the time of its recording it was much more of a glimpse of things to come.

Slates was recorded in February 1981, so naturally by March the group's set was starting to include more material from *Hex Enduction Hour*, on top of songs from the as-yet unreleased mini-LP. The Fall also recorded a session for John Peel on 24th March, which was broadcast on the 31st, three weeks before *Slates* was scheduled to be released. Rather than use the session as an advertisement for their new product, which was the usual practice at the time, The Fall included just one song from *Slates*, 'Middle Mass', preferring instead to debut songs written more recently, including 'Hip Priest'. There was also a jovial re-working of 'The Hucklebuck', an R&B crossover hit from 1949 that had recently reached the UK charts courtesy of Coast to Coast.[22]

One advantage Rough Trade had over Step Forward as a label is that they had a US presence, which meant that *Grotesque* and *Slates* were released in the US at the same time as they were in the UK. This was real progress – *Live at the Witch Trials* had had a delayed release on Miles Copeland's I.R.S. records with a different cover and track listing, and *Dragnet* didn't get an official US release at all.

Access to decent distribution in the States meant that organising a second US tour was now a priority. It was nearly two years

---

[21] It was originally released only on cassette, by Chaos Tapes, a company that specialised in such low-tech releases. Subsequent re-releases in other formats are thus routinely referred to as *The Legendary Chaos Tape*.

[22] The conceit was that we were playing 'C'n'C' from the *Grotesque* album when Mark affected to have learned the tragic news of the assassination of Arthur Askey, and we broke into a spontaneous version (re-christened 'Hassle Schmuk') by way of a tribute. This was a dig at Roxy Music's cover of 'Jealous Guy', which was recorded and released as a tribute to Askey's fellow Liverpudlian John Lennon less than two months after his death. 'Jealous Guy' had been Number 1 in the charts the week before the session was recorded, with '(Do) The Hucklebuck' at Number 5. It was also an example of Mark's astonishing powers of precognition – the 82-year-old Askey died a mere eighteen months after the session was broadcast.

since the group had visited America, and Rough Trade's contacts made organising a tour much easier this time round. As the first tour had been strictly confined to the east and west coasts, Mark and Kay were determined that this trip would be much more comprehensive. They did have one major obstacle to overcome however – obtaining a US work visa for an under-18 to play in venues that were predominantly 21-plus turned out to be pretty much impossible. The only options were putting off the tour till the following February, when I would have turned 18, or getting a stand-in. Given that Karl Burns had recently returned from his self-imposed exile and resumed his position as consigliere, Mark seized the opportunity to give him something to do. At one of our regular Friday afternoon meeting-cum-pay-days in The Foresters Arms,[23] Mark and Kay announced that Karl would be the drummer for the US tour, which was scheduled to start in June. I can't remember being particularly aggrieved, though I must have been disappointed. It did, and still does, make sense, and given my youth and the sheer number of gigs the group played that June and July it would probably have been a wise decision even if work permits hadn't been an issue.

Rather than enter a protracted round of rehearsals (something The Fall were never keen on) it was decided that a short tour of the Netherlands, Belgium and Germany would be an ideal opportunity to break Karl in by having us play alternate nights. The tour started on 9th May in Rotterdam with me behind the kit, while Karl was charged with manning the lights. Karl made his debut in Apeldoorn the next night when the roles were reversed. The fact that the set that night contained not a single song from Karl's original tenure will tell you all you need to know about the group's turnover of material. As the tour progressed Mark occasionally threw in a ragged rendition of 'No Xmas for John Quays', which Karl had played on *Live at the Witch Trials,* but this was just as liable to be on the nights I was the drummer.

[23] Our wages in those days were £25, and Holt's Bitter was about 45p a pint. So at least £2 of the £25 would be spent before The Foresters' towels came on at 3pm. If there was a lock-in till the pub officially re-opened at 5:30pm it was possible to do a quarter of your week's wages in before staggering home some time late Friday evening/Saturday morning.

In fact, The Fall were much more likely to be playing songs from *Hex Enduction Hour*, which wouldn't be released for another ten months, than anything from The Fall's first album. New songs continued to be introduced – as well as 'Jawbone and the Air-Rifle', 'Hip Priest' and 'Winter', the group mapped out 'Fortress' and 'Deer Park' during soundchecks and even included them in the set a couple of times.

I left the tour on the 18th May, just before we got to Berlin – like the US, East Germany wasn't in the habit of allowing minors to perform in drinking establishments. I didn't play with the band again until August.

With Karl now fully broken in and me on extended gardening leave, the group set out on an ambitious US tour barely a week after leaving Germany. The American tour started, as Fall tours usually do, in New York. The gigs the group played on the tour were well documented for the period – a video of 'Totally Wired' from the Mudd Club in New York on 15th June was later included on *Perverted By Language/Bis*, and a live album, culled from various dates on the tour, and entitled *A Part of America Therein, 1981*, was released in 1982.[24]

As well as numerous gigs along the two seaboards, there were dates in Georgia (Atlanta); Tennessee (Memphis); Louisiana (New Orleans); Texas (Houston, Austin and Dallas); Oklahoma (Oklahoma City); Arizona (Phoenix and Tucson) and Illinois (Chicago). It was a proper, full-on American tour and arguably the most extensive The Fall ever undertook. By the end of the tour everyone was firing on all cylinders, apart, of course, from me.

By the time they got back from the US, 'Fortress' and 'Deer Park' had become set regulars, and 'Look, Know' had been arranged but never played. I was hastily introduced to 'Look, Know' (then called 'Know Look') and 'Deer Park' the day before we recorded them for John Peel.[25] That whole day was quite a challenge – the rest of the band had done about 40 gigs with the

[24] Originally a US-only release, the album featured early versions of three of the songs from *Hex Enduction Hour*.
[25] The Fall's fifth session for the *John Peel Show* was recorded on 26th August 1981 and broadcast on 15th September.

best drummer in the world and had played 'Winter' and 'Deer Park' loads of times. As if that wasn't daunting enough we also worked up 'Who Makes The Nazis?' on the spot, from a daft riff Mark had written on his plastic guitar.[26]

Steve Hanley: Mark showed me the song in the loft on his plastic guitar. I thought he was just giving me an idea. I couldn't believe it when he expected me to play it on the session. Who brings a fucking toy guitar to a Peel session?

It was clear the band had evolved while I wasn't there, and Mark was a bit frustrated with my version of 'Winter' in particular. I played it how I remembered it, which was quite loose and behind the beat. With Karl it'd become harder and more nailed on. It wasn't the last time my failure to play like Karl caused a bit of tension.

Between the recording and broadcast of the John Peel session, The Fall played a free gig for the unemployed at Sheffield Polytechnic. This was subsidised by South Yorkshire County Council, so the group still got paid. Eight of the set's thirteen songs were unreleased, including the second encore. The audience were treated to what would become the group's next two singles and half of their next album, none of which had been anywhere near a recording studio at that point. There wasn't room for any previously released A-side either. The only song which could be considered 'old' was 'Put Away', which, thanks to Marc's growing proficiency on the keyboards and everybody's understandable enthusiasm for Karl's drumming, was played as per the Peel version rather than the arrangement that appears on *Dragnet*. I really enjoyed trying to play like Karl on the stuff he'd come up with, though I wasn't really good enough. I was a little more resentful at being asked to be more Burns-like on songs that I considered 'mine'.[27]

---

[26] This was a Selco 'New Beat' toy Beatles guitar, manufactured in 1964 and given to Mark by Kay. It had four strings, so was actually a ukulele in all but name. They're worth about £700 in good nick these days, which of course Mark's wasn't.

[27] I know. Grow up you idiot. It's only drums!

The next event in the group's calendar was a significant one, in many ways: The Fall were booked to play three dates in Iceland. It wasn't unheard of for British bands to play there – The Kinks played in 1965, the early seventies saw Led Zeppelin and Slade perform, The Stranglers had launched their album *Black and White* there in 1978, and The Clash and Any Trouble[28] both played in 1980 – but the arrival of The Fall was still big enough news to make the front of the national newspaper: 'British Raw Rockers Arrive in Iceland'. Perhaps most significantly of all for the group, the visit included the first recordings for what would later become *Hex Enduction Hour*.

---

[28] Netto Elvis Costello & The Attractions. When Marc Riley learned they had been the last UK band to visit Iceland, he apologised to the nation on behalf of the UK.

PART II
HEXEN DEATH BUBBLE

BAWDY LAP-UP
BY LEVI'D U.K. HIRED CAST

The Fall landed at Reykjavik's Keflavik Airport on Tuesday 8th September 1981, to be met by both the national press and a bitter crosswind that tore through our ill-purposed attire. Our entourage consisted of the group, Kay, Grant Showbiz, and Colin Irwin, folk writer for *Melody Maker*, whose jeans-and-a-T-shirt wardrobe was, if anything, even less suited to the arctic conditions than ours. The group's ad-hoc publicist, Versa Manos, had originally put him in touch and he'd made enough of a positive impression on Mark during their interview that he ended up signing on as war correspondent for the whole tour of duty. He was given unprecedented access to the band, and to his credit ended up acting as an unpaid roadie as well as drinking partner and Boswell to Mark's Doctor Johnson.

Colin Irwin: I was a big fan of *Bingo-Master's Break-Out!*, which I'd made *Melody Maker* single of the week. I'd always found Mark convivial, so I was quite open to the idea. The group paid my fare and *Melody Maker* paid my expenses and hotel.

Once immigration had half-heartedly inspected the contents of our battered and frankly unimpressive luggage, the first thing we saw was a sign held against the glass that separated the immigration department from the outside world. It contained just two words: 'Buy Beer'. It was held there by Einar Örn, a local musician and the 'first punk in Iceland' who had discovered The Fall via the car radio.

Einar Örn: I realised that if I parked my mother's Sunbeam car in the right place, on a clear night I could listen to John Peel.

RÓTAÐ Í SKEGGI OG SUKKAÐ Í JARÐARFÖRUM

Mark Smith: „Ætlum að taka upp nokkur lög í Hljóðrita áður en við förum heim til Englands."

30

„Lögin eru mjög einhæf og öll spilamennska er það einnig. Trommuleikarinn er stirður og taktarnir sem hann leikur fjarska einfaldir. Bassistinn og gítarleikararnir tveir endurtaka sömu frasana í sífellu." Þetta hafði einhver tónlistargagnrýnandi um The Fall að segja. Og hann var ekki einn um þá skoðun. Fjöldi manns, sem hlýddi á hljómleika The Fall á Borginni eða í Austurbæjarbíói um síðustu helgi, var á sama máli. En þess ber að minnast að Van Gogh seldi ekki eitt einasta málverk í lífstíð sinni þótt verk hans gangi nú kaupum og sölum á hundruð þúsunda.

Mark E. Smith. — Tónsmíðar

Mark E. Smith — Hlustað í Hljóðrita

„HVERRA FALL"?

Kannski skilja menn ekki samhengið í þessum orðum, það er alltaf þannig með sanna list, hún er sjaldan viðurkennd af samtímanum. Það er framtíðin sem sker úr um gildið. Bach var í rauninni óþekktur kirkjuorganisti þegar hann lést og það var ekki fyrr en á fyrri hluta síðustu aldar að bregða út af hefðbundinni kirkjumúsik að verk hans í dag eru leikin inn á þúsundir hljómplatna.

Og hvernig varð liðsmönnum hljómsveitarinnar The Fall við þessa neikvæðu gagnrýni? Söngvarinn og aðalmaðurinn í The Fall, já einráðurinn sjálfur, sagði: „Þetta eru endalok ferils míns." En hann hló og meinti þetta ekki. Hljómmaður hljómsveitarinnar, gamall pönkleikari sjálfur, hafði um áttið sem birtist hjá gagnrýnendum þetta að segja: „Þegar ég les svona

dóma í breskum blöðum, flýti ég mér alltaf að fara til að sjá viðkomandi hljómsveit, því ég veit að sú hljómsveit sem slíka dóma fær, er að gera eitthvað sérstakt. Eitthvað sem forneskjulegir gagnrýnendurnir hafa hvorki skilið né meðtekið."

Og hvað sögðu the Fall yfirleitt um þessa dóma? Svo sem ekkert, þeir áttu von á þeim. Þeir hafa ekki vanist góðum dómum, þeir eru alltaf að stefna á fullkomleikann. Það sem þeir vóru að eiga við áður er að ryðja sér til rúms fyrst núna hjá öðrum hljómsveitum í Bretlandi.

Mark B. Smith, hinn Bretalegi

(kurtslegi) söngvari og hönnuður The Fall er mjög sérstakur maður og fer sínar eigin leiðir í músíkinni. Hann er algerlega á móti allri sýndarmennsku, þess og hann hefur lýst yfir í lagi því sem hann tók upp í Hljóðrita hf. í Hafnarfirði. Lagið heitir: „You Got to Know What You Look Like, Before You Go Out" og er grín á alla þá sem þykjast vera að mótmæla kerfinu með því einu að klæða sig öðruvísi og skringilega, til að stinga í augun, en eru innst inni aðeins hræddar kirkjurottur sem ekki þora annað en að fylgja nýjustu straumunum, nauðugir viljugir, því hver

Á Hótel Borg

Af hverju er fólk að kaupa plötur okkar ef því líkar ekki tónlistin?

— stölst upp á hótelherbergi Marks Smith, söfuguvara hljómsveitarinnar, og rætt við hann og Kay Carroll, umboðsmann hennar

Jam vinsælust og Fall í mikilli sókn

Haustrokk með The Fall

— breska hljómsveitin The Fall heldur hér þrenna tónleika

PROGRAM

While studying media at Central London Poly he managed to contact Kay Carroll and assure her he could organise a cost-effective and viable trip to Iceland's capital. Impressively, or naively, depending on your point of view, she took him at his word. Einar was a 19-year-old student who turned up without fanfare one day at Rough Trade. But Kay could see he was serious, and against the odds the trip turned out to be a success. She later described it as 'one of my finer and lovelier experiences with The Fall'.

A quick discussion with the locals revealed the meaning behind Einar's cryptic instruction: the airport's duty-free shop was the last place to buy beer before entering the country.[29] Steve, Craig, Marc and I divvied up what little money we had and bought 24 beers between us. They didn't last the first afternoon.

Craig Scanlon: We had half of Iceland in our hotel room, trying to sample the forbidden fruit – cans of Carlsberg.

The Fall being what they were, Mark and Kay went off to dinner while the rest of the group, with Einar and Colin Irwin in tow, were despatched to collect the stage from where it was being stored to transport and then erect it at the venue ahead of the following night's gig. For the most part, we didn't have much of a problem with this, it was just the way things were.[30]

[29] In 1935, when Iceland voted to end prohibition, it was argued that as beer was cheaper, it was more likely to be drunk to excess, and so remained illegal. The absurdity of this argument was lost on no one, but the ban lasted a further fifty-four years. It was only when increased tourism exposed it to the ridicule of the rest of the world that the law was finally rescinded.

[30] For the tour of the UK and the Netherlands in March-April 1982, Mark and Kay did a deal with the legendary Oz PA company, who consisted of Keith 'Oz' McCormick, Diane Barton and Eddie Hallam. It was agreed that the group's backline would travel in the PA truck and we would act as their unpaid roadies in return for a reduced rate on PA hire. As we had no techs of our own, this meant we were helping them hump the PA and the backline into the venue, setting it up on stage, soundchecking, doing the gig, dismantling everything and finally loading out the backline and the PA and helping them pack the truck. When we played Edinburgh Nite Club on 2nd April 1982, we were delighted to discover it was conveniently located on the top floor of the Edinburgh Playhouse, six flights up. According to author Ian Rankin, it's possible Detective John Rebus attended this gig, though I don't remember seeing him. Tales of Oz PA's legendary exploits are woven into the fabric of Manchester's post-punk music scene, and there really should be a book about them.

Craig Scanlon: I remember reading that we'd built the stage, but I don't remember doing it. Maybe I shirked out.

Colin Irwin: The band seemed to be absolutely terrified of Mark, who in turn was quite wary of Kay. Whenever they had something to discuss, Marc Riley seemed to act as their spokesman.

The article Colin Irwin eventually wrote for *Melody Maker* was a refreshingly breezy piece of reportage – quite different from other articles published around the same time. Much of the difference came from the fact that Irwin spent time around the whole group rather than sequestered away with Mark.

Colin Irwin: It was a strange place, especially in those days. On top of it being permanently light it seemed like every bar was full of trawlermen desperate to pick a fight.

Mark was unimpressed with the article as published, particularly the way it shone daylight on the supposed magic of The Fall's creative process. Irwin's article revealed that The Fall, like every other group, depended as much on perspiration as inspiration. If that was true, then Mark was determined that there be no doubt as to who provided each. On the sleeve notes to *Hex* he highlighted the fact that his calling was somewhat higher than the rest of us:

> White face Finds Roots, boys don't even notice & look
> for games machines.

In fact, the real take-away from the article was the band's utter determination to realise Mark's vision, and how often this required us to steadfastly ignore the fact that he didn't think we were up to it.

There was quite a lot crammed into the short trip. We played two gigs at the Hotel Borg, the basement of which was now performance ready, thanks to our efforts the previous night. Both gigs were notably well-attended, and by a surprising cross-section of the Icelandic population.

Colin Irwin: After the gig I got chatting to someone who I later found out was Björk. I said to Einar that she seemed a little strange and he replied that everyone in Iceland was a little strange.

Marc Riley: It was so bleak there. There was no tourism. And the mentality of the Icelandic people was like that of The Fall, to be honest. It was a real case of us versus them. They were out on a limb. Iceland didn't integrate. It was a really strange community of people. They were really nice but otherworldly.

Support on the second night came from Q4U, a bizarre local punk band whose lead singer insisted on removing most of her attire, to general audience indifference. Thankfully she wasn't in attendance for the third gig as it was a matinee with a crowd that contained a significant number of children.

Mark E. Smith: Iceland was a closed country, not like it is now. They didn't have rock bands and beer was illegal and stuff like that. So we did a show there and it was a big deal for them. It was ridiculous; a quarter of the population of Rekyjavik turned out to see us.

Following our triumphs at the Hotel Borg, the next day, 11th September 1981, saw me nursing the worst hangover I had ever experienced in my young life. I clearly couldn't cope with a spirits-only alcohol regime, and I wasn't the only one.[31]

Mark E. Smith: You could only drink shit like pints of peach schnapps. I remember firing into it one day and night. I thought my legs had been stolen afterwards.[32]

---

[31] As it happens, the only time I ever had one worse was also with The Fall. It was the result of an end-of-weekend celebratory trip to a disco in Greece. The weekend had seen The Birthday Party, The Fall and New Order play on consecutive nights at a basketball stadium in Athens. The gigs were all sold out, so the delighted promoter insisted on furnishing all three bands with an endless, and free, supply of Ouzo. I have, quite correctly, avoided the noxious brew ever since. On the flight home the next day, Craig, who was even worse than me, stated, 'If the pilot announces he's decided to fly the plane into the side of a mountain I'll give him a round of applause.'

[32] To be fair I don't think they made you drink *pints* of schnapps – they were metric for a start.

Mark, who could well have been a little delicate himself, was less than sympathetic towards my self-induced ill-health, and he wasted no time letting me know the depths of his disappointment. As I was already feeling a little insecure in my position, it made for a less than convivial atmosphere for our scheduled trip to the recording studio.

[SIDE ONE: TRACK 3] Hip Priest

Words: Smith **Music:** Hanley (S)-Hanley (P)-Riley-Scanlon-Smith (Smith/The Fall)[33]

Smith vocal; *Riley* guitar, keyboards; *Scanlon* guitar, vocal; *Hanley (S)* bass; *Hanley (P)* drums; *Carroll* glockenspiel

First played live: 17th March 1981, Riley-Smith Hall, Leeds University

Recorded: 11th September 1981, Hljóðriti studio, Reykjavík, Iceland[34]

Producers: Grant Showbiz, Mark E. Smith. **Engineer:** Tony Cook[35]

Released: 8th March 1982

[33] All the songwriting credits in this book come from the Performing Rights Society database. This is the important one, as it determines who actually gets paid. For comparison, I've included the credits as printed on the label of the original vinyl pressing in brackets. Of course it's often the case that neither accurately reflects who actually wrote what. Sometimes they're just what Mark felt like putting at the time. As Craig points out, 'He's left us a great legacy of arguing. He'd be laughing his head off about that.' He's got a point. The music for 'Wings', possibly Craig's greatest guitar line, is credited to Smith/Hanley (S).

[34] Opened in 1975 by Vilhjálmur Vilhjálmsson, Hljóðriti had been used by nearly all of Iceland's recording artists including a pre-Sugarcubes Björk.

[35] Tony Cook first worked as an engineer for Polydor UK in the early seventies, where one of his projects was the recording of *Neil Sedaka Live at The Royal Festival Hall* with the Royal Philharmonic Orchestra. He moved to Iceland in 1975 and was heavily involved with Hljóðriti's development. He was responsible for hundreds of recording sessions there between 1975 and 1984, including many of Björk's early sessions. He had no reason to be impressed by the northern oiks he was presented with in September 1981, and he really wasn't.

BIG P.

It was a fortuitous decision to record 'Hip Priest' in Iceland. Obviously, in a country with such a small population, recording facilities were in short supply. As a result, Hljóðriti was more upmarket than we were used to, and due to its unique location in a cave formed by lava flows, it was also markedly atmospheric. In short, it was a mix of tangible technology and ethereal ambiance.

Craig Scanlon: Because it says it was recorded in a cave I can imagine everyone thinks it was dank with water dripping off the walls. But it was a plush, beautiful studio with a big Steinway grand piano, which I immediately homed in on.

Given that everyone was keen to use our limited time in the studio to continue the aural trajectory of recent sessions, it was perfect. Grant in particular was keen to show that he had more in his armoury than the jarring auditory assault that he had applied to *Dragnet*. While Adrian Sherwood had embraced the idea of 'anti-production' following his experience working on *Slates*, Grant was moving in the opposite direction.

Grant Showbiz: Inevitably, my approach to recording and mic position was evolving. Having built my own studio at the tail end of 1979,[36] I'd become slightly more friendly with Mr Reverb. Also I think you can chart a different style of studio use through *Dragnet*, *Grotesque*, *Slates* and into *Hex*. *Slates* in particular had influenced how I felt about studios through the presence of Adrian Sherwood, who seemed to delight in the whole process, and his obvious glee at manipulating sound was infectious.

[36] Street-Level, where The Fall had recorded 'Pay Your Rates' and 'The Container Drivers' for *Grotesque*. Grant started the studio with Kif Kif Le Batteur (aka Keith Dobson, though rather sweetly Discogs.com lists his real name as 'Frank Honest') and José Gross from Here & Now.

Grant wasted no time in utilising his newly-honed production and engineering skills and took a decidedly hands-on approach to setting up for the day ahead. This was fortunate as his level of enthusiasm was more than matched by the English in-house engineer's indifference to our requirements.

Grant Showbiz: Much more time was used in setting up and positions of mics. I wanted to make sure Mark was slightly tethered in his ability to roam the studio, and that there was a bit more separation of instruments. The dear old engineer, as ever, was fairly perplexed by it all.

As captured on tape on 11th September, 'Hip Priest' remains one of the group's most successful recordings. Despite a pointedly uninterested engineer, as a studio, Hljóðriti especially suited the song's delicate approach. Its high-end facilities also allowed for a degree of finesse that some of the later songs on *Hex* wouldn't require.

Grant Showbiz: I always say that telling the engineer that what appeared to be some musicians rambling around, tuning, and generally fiddling, was actually 'Hip Priest', and that he should start the tape machine, was one of my greatest achievements.

By the time it was recorded, 'Hip Priest' had been a regular part of The Fall's set for six months. Given that its surprisingly disciplined structure comes entirely from dynamics rather than chord changes or riffs, this relatively long gestation period was exactly what the song needed. It was built around a drum beat which was an unlikely marriage of what Mark always referred to as a 'cabaret-beat'[37] and the mournful Manchester rhythm utilised so effectively by Steve Morris on Joy Division's 'New Dawn Fades'.

[37] More properly referred to as a 'Shuffle beat', it's often heard in country and western (where it's sometimes called a 'Ray Price shuffle') and ballroom swing. It was first introduced to The Fall by Mike Leigh on 'Fiery Jack' and crowbarred at Mark's insistence into 'The N.W.R.A.'. It wasn't really utilised by any other new wave act until 'The Love Cats' by The Cure.

'Hip Priest' was first ad-libbed at the soundcheck for a gig at Leeds University on 17th March 1981. In *The Big Midweek* Steve described the process by which the music developed as a kind of communal experience, with the four of us 'nurturing it with our tempered anguish'. The arrangement, such as it was in that early incarnation, was worked up using nothing more than unschooled intuition and the odd furtive glance. Sensing that this improvisation had the potential to develop into something singularly striking, Mark included 'Hip Priest' in the set the same night. Highly unusually for the time, the gig was captured for posterity on video, and given that the song had not existed in any form at all until a few hours earlier, the video offers an unparalleled glimpse into The Fall's writing process. Though this first run out sounds like we're groping our way out of the dark and building the song from virtually nothing, Mark was adamant this wasn't the case.

Mark E. Smith: I wrote 'Hip Priest'. Were they capable of writing something like 'J. Temperance' or 'Hip Priest'? You've got to be joking. Just look at what they've done afterwards.

While a version recorded for John Peel a week after the Leeds gig shows some significant signs of progress, particularly in the lyric, the song still had some way to go before it was complete. Further evolution can be detected in the version released on *A Part of America Therein*, which was recorded live in Chicago on 16th July 1981.[38] In some ways it's a shame that the song's development is so well documented. The final recorded version is so satisfying in its dynamism and perfect rendering of Mark's lyric, it's almost diminished by one's ability to see the workings.

Decidedly sparse, especially when compared with the later material on *Hex*, 'Hip Priest' was mainly recorded live, the only overdubs being Mark's second vocal, Kay's glockenspiel and a re-recording of the bass drum ordered by Mark as he felt the

---

[38] According to Karl, at one stage Mark favoured this version for inclusion on *Hex* instead of the Iceland version. With hindsight, this seems more likely to be one of the many occasions where Karl was messing with me.

original was slightly hesitant.[39] Craig did his backing vocals, and Marc switched from guitar – which he played up to the first crescendo – to keyboards in the same take. He'd recently augmented the Elgam Snoopy electric piano,[40] which provides the sound of the Hip Priest's tobacco-ravaged breaths at the end of the song, with a Diamond 600 organ. The organ was much more versatile and massively more intense-sounding than the Snoopy. Its introduction added a new dimension to the group's sound, not least in its capability to play sustained notes.

What's most striking about 'Hip Priest' musically is its sheer difference from the rest of the group's material at the time. While many songs on *Hex* ('Winter'; 'And This Day'; 'Deer Park') feature extended extemporising around a single riff, 'Hip Priest' takes this one further by dispensing with even that. It exists without the safety net of either a clear chord structure or a recurrent bassline. Given the self-taught musicians involved, that it achieved such a level of coherence while retaining its fragility is entirely down to its extended evolution on the live stage. Unlike some other Fall songs, it wasn't committed to vinyl until it was ready. It could almost be described as jazz, if that didn't come with the unwanted baggage of a sense of improvisation for improvisation's sake.

Craig Scanlon: We really did know that song, not to the point where it became stale, but we knew where to leave stuff and just stop dead.

The lyric mirrors the music by also dovetailing from the rest of the album. In this case it's by being uniquely unguarded, once you

[39] With Mark still pining for Karl, my drumming was under abnormally close scrutiny.
[40] The original Elgam Snoopy was purchased by Una and passed to Yvonne, who played it on *Witch Trials*. Marc inherited it from her and used it for the first time on 'How I Wrote Elastic Man'. By the time we recorded 'Hip Priest', two years of intense touring had taken its toll and it wasn't capable of much more than wheezes. Marc purchased an exact replica, which he took with him as part of his severance pay when he left The original Snoopy was then resurrected and used on 'The Man Whose Head Expanded' and *Perverted By Language*. It appeared for the last time (played by me) on the verses of *The Wonderful and Frightening World of The Fall*'s 'Slang King', where unsurprisingly it makes a sort of wheezy breath sound.

accept that the Hip Priest is Mark. In fact, Mark's conviction that appreciation for what he was trying to do was in such short supply and would only worsen over the coming months, he considered breaking up the group, or at least retroactively affected to have considered it.

When pressed on the sombre nature of the words in contemporary interviews, Mark attempted, as always, to deflect attention away from the personal.

Mark E. Smith: It was a bit of a joke on the group cos they're all like Catholics ... it's meant to be a bit of a funny song ... I have an image of Johnny Cash or somebody, I don't know why ... or South America.

The song's protagonist sharing some DNA with Johnny Cash gave Mark free rein to reference one of his favourite songs – 'Sunday Morning Coming Down' – a Kris Kristofferson song that Cash recorded for his TV show and released as a single in 1970. The line 'I got my last clean dirty shirt outta the wardrobe' is a paraphrasing of 'Sunday Morning's 'I fumbled in my closet through my clothes, and found my cleanest dirty shirt' and the protagonist of both songs share a similar world-weariness and sense of loss. Both characters, alienated and cast adrift from the rest of the populace by virtue of their time on the road, waste no time getting stuck into the brown bottles. And it's not difficult to see why Mark saw something of himself in Kristofferson's anti-hero.

The 'Hip' part of the title is a pun, referring both to the hipster-priest type that Mark casts himself as, and also as an acronym for 'hypnotic induction process', a phrase, referring to the act of putting someone under hypnosis, that Mark uses in the lyric to 'Just Step S'ways' and on the version of 'Hip Priest' captured on *A Part of America Therein*. This is possibly also the source of the made-up word 'Enduction' in the album's title.

'Drink the long draught Dan' has more than an echo of a line from Charlotte Brontë's *Jane Eyre* – 'I rose, bathed my head and face in water, drank a long draught' – but one of the more interesting discussions about the song amongst Fall devotees is the idea that the 'Dan' referred to is actually Danny Baker. Baker was an early champion of The Fall who nonetheless had no qualms about criticising the group when he felt they required it. The theory is based around a live review Baker wrote for *ZigZag* in 1978 which contains the following phrases:

> There is no anger on the band's part just a sort of dry disgust. Nothing to do with 'you should appreciate us' thinking but a sort of what is the fucking point? Maybe the only thing is to appeal to your sense of cultishness (!) and say it's hip to see them before they get big.

The use of 'appreciate' and 'hip' notwithstanding, it's worth reminding ourselves that we're mainly working backwards from Mr Baker's first name, though it's as good a theory as any.

As with 'The N.W.R.A.', 'Hip Priest's narration shifts halfway through. This time the song starts in the third person, introducing the Hip Priest with the line 'He's gonna make an appearance', at which point the Hip Priest takes over and speaks for himself. His first revelation, that he was 'shown in a freakshow', is perfectly emphasised by Marc's queasy fairground organ.

Of course, Mark attempts to deflect the idea that he's giving anything away. At the end, once all that remains of the feast is a tray of grease, Mark would like us to believe that he's left no trace of himself behind.

Mark E. Smith: I'm not a private person but I don't want everyone to know everything if you know what I mean.

He has, he tells us, emerged from the song unscathed, with clean hands.[41] But it's less true of this song than most other Fall songs, as he admitted in 1981:

[41] 'I'm as clean as a packet of chocolate Treets' refers to a 1980s TV commercial for Mars' confectionary Treets which were marketed with the slogan 'melt in your mouth, not in your hand'. Mark clearly had one eye on the telly ads while composing – 'Step S'ways' mentions 'a Hovis advert' and 'The Classical' takes issue with the commercial

Mark E. Smith: That gets a bit personal at times. Maybe a bit too personal.

Craig Scanlon: Mark sometimes used to get his friend, Gerard, who was an actor, on stage to do the 'I'm a Hip Priest' bit, because it was so personal.

In fact, Mark identified with this Hip Priest figure so completely that he later reused the lyric. The nearest thing The Fall ever came to a theme song, 'Big New Prinz', was also one of the group's most-played numbers.[42] As noted by Richard Osborne in 'The Fall on Vinyl', a chapter in *Mark E. Smith and The Fall: Art, Music and Politics,* the ambiguity with regards to the identity of the Hip Priest on record is obliterated in performance.

> As for the identity of the 'Hip Priest', this is [a] song in which the narrative fluctuates: Smith sings of the Hip Priest, and he sings as the Hip Priest. As so often with his song's characters, doubt remains as to the degree of self-portrayal. Nevertheless, in live performances of recent years the main refrain of 'Big New Prinz' has taken on a more concrete meaning. The audience knows that Smith is the Hip Priest and, although adored by his loyal following, this latent national institution accepts the call-and-response refrain that it is 'he' who 'is not appreciated'.

Because of this close association between its eponymous hero and Mark E. Smith himself, 'Hip Priest' has enjoyed a profile and a place in the public domain far beyond what one might expect for a radio-unfriendly album track. It was the only song used in Michael Clark's prestigious Sadler's Wells ballet *I Am Curious,*

for Wilkinson Sword's 'Profile' disposable razor. 'Suits Off, Jeans On' which appears on *Hex*'s sleeve, and on the Peel version of 'C'n'C', was from the 1979 jingle for Townsend Thoresen ferries. Mark would use his ear for a snappy strapline again in 1983 on 'Eat Y'self Fitter', this time using an advert for Kellogg's Bran Flakes as the source.

[42] 'Big New Prinz' was played live 213 times. It made its debut at the first performance of Michael Clark's ballet *I Am Curious, Orange* (which featured The Fall and where it was segued with 'Hip Priest') in June 1988 and its final outing was in Switzerland in March 2006. Note that Mark never felt the need to perform the song with The Fall's final two line-ups, both of which he spoke of with nothing but praise right up until his death. Maybe it was finished business, and he finally felt properly appreciated.

Orange that wasn't written specifically for it. As well as being the title for the first serious biography of Mark and The Fall, 'Hip Priest' was the go-to sub-heading for Mark's many obituaries. It is, of course, the Fall song that most people have heard, though many of them won't have realised it. 'Hip Priest's tale of the strange outsider who refuses to reveal his inner self was later used very effectively in the film *The Silence of the Lambs*, a 1991 adaptation of Thomas Harris's novel of the same name. In the film, the song and presumably the album is a personal favourite of Jame Gumb, the tailor-cum serial killer 'Buffalo Bill', who likes to play it while he sews.[43] In fact it was included in the film's soundtrack on the insistence of its director, Jonathan Demme, who was a long-time admirer of the group.[44]

Jonathan Demme: There may have been a couple of bands as good as The Fall in the last 20 years, but nobody's been better.

The song is heard under the movie's climactic cat-and-mouse scene, when the junior FBI agent Clarice Starling, played by Jodie Foster, finally comes fact to face with the psychotic killer. It's never heard clearly – the way it fades in and out is used to great effect to highlight Starling's disorientation as the cellar is plunged into total darkness – but it's unmistakably The Fall.

Marc Riley: The thing with 'Hip Priest' is that it was always tentative. It didn't matter how many times we played it, it always had that feeling of 'when's it going to kick off?' It's no coincidence a serial killer ends up listening to it.

Mark was approached in 1990 for permission to use the track, and agreed after the group's then manager, Trevor Long, negotiated an advance payment to the current group of £6000.

---

[43] Played brilliantly by Ted Levine.
[44] Jonathan Demme was a highly successful Hollywood director who also made live documentaries for Talking Heads (*Stop Making Sense*), Justin Timberlake (*Justin Timberlake & The Tennessee Kids*) and several for Neil Young, as well as music videos for Bruce Springsteen and New Order. He died in April 2017.

But he was eternally resentful that the song's credits meant that the songwriting royalties later accrued from the film went directly to the members of the group at the time it was recorded, rather than to him. Particularly when *The Silence of the Lambs* turned out to be one of the most successful films of 1991, and garnered a number of awards, including a Best Director Oscar for Demme. And it's still earning money for the writers of 'Hip Priest' today.

Mark E. Smith: It's odd with stuff like films and adverts. You don't get much money for it. I'm quite funny about that ... As soon as people see it on the telly all the ex-members dive in demanding a share. I wrote all of 'Sparta' and I wrote 'Hip Priest' but every time *The Silence of the Lambs* is shown on TV, which it's used in, the royalties go six ways, [so] you end up with only about 8%.[45] [...] I could have had a mansion by now, but it doesn't bother me.[46]

Craig Scanlon: It was great seeing your name on the big screen. It was nice of Mark giving that song to us, wasn't it?

[45] Just to clear this up, and hopefully without any suggestion that the real split is unfair, the song is credited to Smith/Riley/Scanlon/Hanley (S)/Hanley (P). However, the actual split is 50% for the lyric (which obviously all went to Mark) and 50% for the music, which was split equally between all 5 of us. So Mark actually got 60% and the rest of us 10%. This 50% words, 50% music split is usually the way The Fall's credits work, but not always.
[46] In fact Mark was so sanguine about the songwriting credits on 'Hip Priest' that he made sure he pointed out just how much it didn't bother him over several interviews.

[SIDE TWO: TRACK 4] **Iceland**

Words: Smith **Music:** Hanley (S)-Riley-Scanlon-Smith
(Smith/Scanlan[47]/Riley/Hanley S)

Smith vocal, cassette, guitar; *Riley* banjo; *Scanlon* piano; *Hanley (S)* bass;
Hanley (P) drums; *Carroll* percussion

First played live: 12th September 1981, Austurbaejarbio, Reykjavik,
Iceland

Recorded: 11th September 1981, Hljóðriti studio, Reykjavík, Iceland

Producer: Grant Showbiz. **Engineer:** Tony Cook

Released: 8th March 1982

---

[47] Craig's surname was routinely misspelled for the first few years of his tenure.

Casting Runes

After successfully committing 'Hip Priest' to tape in fairly short order, the group moved on to 'Look, Know'. As it turned out, this version wasn't particularly successful, mainly because we'd only played it live a couple of times and Marc's counter-point vocal had yet to be added.

Mark decided to use the remaining studio time to compose, rehearse, record and mix an entirely new song. This was to be based around a lyric he had just written, which, as usual, he saw no need to share with the rest of the group. The only clue the musicians had when attempting to conjure up the appropriate atmosphere was the vaguely disquieting sounds Mark had captured on his ever-present cassette recorder.

It's often been argued, and with some degree of credibility, that Mark E. Smith's ability to identify which band members were past their best or no longer pulling their weight and unsentimentally dispense with their services was one of The Fall's greatest strengths. However, Mark's fondness for tampering with the formula doesn't alter the fact that some of the group's finest releases came during periods of relative stability. This is certainly the case for *Hex Enduction Hour*. Mark, Marc, Craig and Steve had been playing and writing together for nearly three years by the time of its release, and it's their untutored cohesiveness which more than anything else made *Hex* such a satisfying body of work. It's certainly what enabled them to compose a piece like 'Iceland', a song whose music almost exactly captured the tangible atmosphere of a lyric they had never heard before they started playing. While there's no denying that there was an element of luck to this – after all they were never really able to do it again – it's unlikely that any other set of musicians could have done a better job.

Craig Scanlon: You have these accounts of us in the studio going 'Ooo what are we going to do?' and Mark saying 'just get a fucking tune done'. But I loved the opportunity to do that.

In *Mark E. Smith and The Fall: Art, Music and Politics* Robin Purves devotes a whole essay to 'Iceland's improvised origins. He begins by correctly identifying the track as an example of 'idiomatic' improvisation rather than the 'free' improvisation favoured by such notable improv musicians as Derek Bailey.[48] For a start the 'democratic space' that Bailey would have us believe is an essential part of free improv was not always forthcoming in Fall recording sessions. There was always someone looking over your shoulder.

Even so, and despite Colin Irwin's understandable first impressions of the group's dynamic, the group were far more than what Mark Fisher calls 'the zombie slaves of [Smith's] vision'. As Robin Purves pointed out:

> The boys in the band, who, much to their own credit, are more interested in playing Space Invaders than in conjuring their own epiphanies of ethnicity, are key to the song and its success. The sound of the song exactly characterizes the state of the rapport between the singer and the rest of the band; the lyrics comment upon their relations; 'Iceland' is about the intra-group tensions and alliances and it enacts them in a way that is immeasurably more nuanced that the familiar descriptions of Smith as martinet and the rest of the group as hapless drones. ... The singer is granted the opportunity to weather the risk of exposure in the act of improvisation and then to slip almost unnoticed from the track, as the group ... improvise an extended instrumental passage of harsh beauty and sensitivity unlike any other in the corpus of The Fall.

[48] Bailey was an avant-garde ('French for bullshit', to quote John Lennon, though he later changed his mind under the influence of Yoko Ono) electric guitarist and a leading figure in the aforementioned free improvisation movement, which favoured noise and atonality over melody and structure. A right bleeding racket, by all accounts.

Marc Riley: He said he wanted a song like Bob Dylan, so we wrote the music to 'Iceland' – which doesn't even sound like a Dylan song – and I mentioned this in an interview once and he went bonkers. He didn't want that wall to be broken down, he didn't want any of that stuff to be revealed to anyone else. I mean, the song is a kind of a folk song and is about us being in Iceland, and it doesn't even sound like Dylan, but he went bonkers.

Craig Scanlon: It's a very un-Mark Smith thing to say about Dylan. He wouldn't mention Bob Dylan in any interview. He never gave any secrets away. But he must have said it, because I was trying to capture 'come gather round people' on the piano while Marc was doing this brilliant thing on the banjo. Because it was recorded so quickly you can hear me still figuring out how to go up. We always had to try and keep mistakes to a minimum because as soon as anything was recorded it was out of our hands. You just let your song go and left it to Mark, and a lot of the time, production-wise it was really good. But he spent a lot of time working his vocals, and we didn't have that luxury.

It sounded so good that Steve and I were initially at a loss as to what we could add, a fact which Mark picked up on and filed away for later use. It didn't take us long to work it out, though. Freed from his usual obligation to provide a bedrock, Steve added a subtle line that echoed the distracted nature of the lyric. The drums were easy after that – I just recreated the relentless pounding in my head that Iceland's ridiculous licensing laws had helpfully provided.

The change in instrumentation was significant, as it meant everyone approached the recording in a different way. It became a piece of work in its own right, rather than a preparation for live performance, which was the group's usual mindset when new material was hammered out.[49] No one was thinking beyond the moment, and the ease with which it came together is probably

[49] Mark was so moved by this temporary spirit of extemporisation that he overdubbed two electric guitar parts of his own over the extended outro, effectively duetting with himself.

what convinced Mark to try a similar approach on the *Room To Live* sessions some months later. But if the resultant record shows anything, it's that such fortuitous lightning rarely strikes twice. In truth, the uniquely spontaneous air of 'Iceland' was never successfully revisited by the line-up that recorded it.

Colin Irwin: I was sitting next to Mark on the bus that was taking us to the studio. In between chatting he was scribbling down odd bits of text as they came to him. I was amazed when they turned out to be the lyrics to the song they recorded later the same day, 'Iceland'.

Lyrically, the way 'Iceland' see-saws between reportage and Norse saga reflects the mood of both the *Melody Maker* article and the trip itself – the mixture of the mystic and mundane that is the day-to-day reality of a writer who is also a touring performer. Mark's ability to encompass both of these disciplines in a single song is part of what made him such an unusual lyricist – it's difficult to imagine many writers who could combine an anecdote about slipping on their arse in a café with a quasi-Norse saga of godmen walking amongst us. A similar melding of the preternatural and the prosaic can be found in the line 'Memorex for the krakens'.[50] Mark had already mentioned the monstrous sea creatures in the lyric to 'Winter', possibly referencing Lovecraft's *The Call of Cthulhu*. Given the kraken's origins in Norse mythology it's tempting to imagine him capturing their unworldly cries on his miniature tape-recorder in his hotel room and using the recording as the basis for the song.[51]

The song's bathetic juxtapositions are probably best summed up in the lines 'Cast the runes against your own soul – Roll up for the underpants show'. Whether it's contemplating the fleeting nature of your life when set against an ancient and epic backdrop, or having customs hold up your skiddies for all to see, there's evidently more than one way to be humbled in Iceland. The lyric

[50] Memorex was a brand of audio cassette that was heavily advertised at the time.
[51] It was probably the heating. But then again you always think it's the pipes till it turns on the lights.

also references Mark's discovery of Megas – Magnús Þór Jónsson – a maverick Icelandic folk singer who had ceased performing by the time The Fall arrived in Iceland. Mark obviously felt some kinship with the singer; he rarely name-checked other artists without adding some form of at-least-oblique criticism. Colin Irwin's *Melody Maker* article records the fact that Megas turned up at one of the gigs, and was introduced to Mark, though not to anyone else in the band. In an interview with *The Reykjavik Grapevine* ahead of the group's return to Iceland in 2013, for some bizarre reason Mark denied they had ever met.[52] It's possible he was disappointed with the actual person when compared to the legendary figure he had eulogised in song, in which case the contrast between man and myth is a neat parallel to the rest of the lyric.

Encompassing three sold-out gigs and two of the group's most satisfying recordings, The Fall's trip to Iceland could be viewed as one of their most successful ventures to date. No wonder Mark was keen to shake things up as soon as he got home.

Steve Hanley: The Iceland recording was one of the best things we did, but you had Mark shouting about 'wasting time' and playing up for the press. I don't know why he felt he had to do that, or mess with our amps. Maybe he was insecure.

Marc Riley: Mark had this over-inflated working-class ideology about how everyone should work hard. Except he didn't work hard.

Many attempts to sum up Mark's attitude to his group, particularly after his death, have made a point of comparing Mark to James Brown, ostensibly because of quotes like this: 'I like to make sure they know from the start that The Fall is a job of work like any other. It's the same deal whether you're playing to 20 or 20,000. Discipline, that's what counts.' Of course, what they failed to note, as Angus McDonald has pointed out, is that

[52] The meeting was confirmed by Colin when interviewed for this book.

'James Brown was as ferociously professional as he expected his band-employees to be. Put mildly, this has not always been the case with Smith.'

Unusually for a Fall song, 'Iceland' never became a part of the live set.

Craig Scanlon: We tried it once, but we gave it up after two minutes. Trying to recreate a Steinway on a Snoopy electric piano was never going to work.

K.K.AMERA – FOGEY LABEL

Now that the ground-breaking trips to the USA and Iceland were complete, the focus fully shifted to the next single and LP. With three songs recorded, and half a dozen other new songs making regular appearances in our set, the group had every reason to be confident that the next album would be a good one. But, unbeknownst to the rest of us, Mark was harbouring some uncharacteristic doubts.

Mark E. Smith: I went into it thinking that it was the last thing we'd ever do because we were getting nowhere. You've got to put it in the period it was in, you know: New Romantics, indie, gloomy music. So I thought, 'This is our last chance to put a proper LP out.' [...] When you're mired in the shit of the times you start to question not only people's tastes but their existences. You're not going anywhere with all that shit.

Craig Scanlon: It's a drama queen moment from Mark – we knew nothing about it being the last album. We certainly didn't play like it was the last thing we'd do. I think that was his little Walter Mitty moment.

Steve Hanley: He only ever said it in interviews afterwards. I think he was rewriting history.

Marc Riley: What would he have done? What he did was amazing, but he needed a band, and I can't see him getting up and nine o'clock in the morning and writing a book, he didn't have the discipline.

Craig Scanlon: In his head he thought he should be a writer, but he wasn't a novelist, he was great lyricist.

If the next album was going to be the last thing The Fall would ever do, Mark was determined to create something entirely on his own terms.[53] With that in mind, the first item of business was which label he trusted to release it. The Fall and Rough Trade had never been a particularly good fit, as Steve Jameson, the Rough Trade staffer who'd instigated Mark and Kay's initial discussions with Geoff Travis, admitted:

Steve Jameson: I persuaded Mark E. Smith to go there with The Fall. I had lots of conversations with him about it and his basic line was, 'I'm not signing with that bunch of amateur college wankers.'

Jameson rightly pointed out to Mark that Rough Trade's amateur nature meant a much more favourable deal than would be forthcoming from a major label.

Mark E. Smith: The initial beauty in Rough Trade was the contract, fifty to them and fifty to the group, which was very innovative at the time.

But despite the obvious financial advantages, Mark and Kay were deeply suspicious of Rough Trade's seemingly egalitarian set up, with things coming to a head after the release of *Slates*.

Mark E. Smith: They didn't like the sentiment behind some of the records ... they'd always have people interfering. ... They wanted lyrics to all the songs and stuff like that – it was like living in Russia. […] We stuck with 'em as long as we could, I'd just had enough of fucking idiots who'd been working there for about three weeks, fucking socialist art student never done a day's work in his fucking life, coming up and telling me what he thought would be a good idea for the record. I'd rather hear it coming from a fat executive. […] *Slates* was the final straw. They didn't want to bring it out because it was a 10-inch; neither an album

---

[53] The group's schedule was particularly punishing in the period following *Hex*'s release, so someone was still planning ahead.

nor a single. I wanted to release something that could be bought by the working man. Geoff Travis and his ilk were only arsed about entertaining their mates round the corner. [...] It was none of their business, so I walked.

Kay Carroll: The gist of it for me was it felt like they had lost their personal edge. Geoff Travis was now delegating A&R people towards us, there seemed a complacency and an arrogance overall, and that definitely wasn't there when we first started all collaborating together. I didn't want to be treated as a prima donna, quite the contrary, I just wanted respect, authenticity and integrity for both me and the band. The last couple of meetings with Rough Trade felt like a revisiting of Virgin Records, who epitomized everything I hated about the music business.[54] Mark pretty much echoed my feelings too, that it was time for a change ... see ya mate!

Mark E. Smith: They were always alright with us, it's just that we were a part of that fucking morass of untalented groups, we were just being treated the same as other groups, and we're not like that, we're better than all that other shit.

Mark and Kay discussed their next steps with publicist Versa Manos. She suggested they speak to her downstairs neighbour, Chris Youle, who had just started his own record label. Mark was immediately impressed, both by the prospective label's access to finance, and by their willingness to spend it how the group saw fit, both of which set them apart from Rough Trade.

Mark E. Smith: They'd just made a load of dosh from the *Grease* soundtrack album. Old-fashioned rockers – out every night in London.

---

[54] Kay had dealings with Virgin when negotiating the release of *Short Circuit*, a live compilation album from the last nights of Collyhurst's Electric Circus. It featured two tracks by The Fall, 'Last Orders' and 'Stepping Out'.

Chris Youle: Prior to starting Kamera I worked for RCA, Polydor International and then as MD of RSO Records, where I worked with Eric Clapton, The Bee Gees, Freddie King and Paul Nicholas, amongst others.[55] The last album I released before Stigwood kicked me out was *Saturday Night Fever*.[56] After RSO I started Acrobat Records whose main acts were Roger Chapman from Family, and Dollar. Acrobat collapsed but I carried on managing Roger Chapman. I needed office space and an old friend, Steve Melhuish, offered me space above his record shop, Bonaparte, in Kings Cross. Bonaparte had a big export department specialising in punk and indie labels. Steve decided to start his own label, Human, which I ran for him. Signings included Zeitgeist, Hermine, The Slits and Au Pairs. We used independent pressing plants and another old friend of mine, Eric Parsons, did all the sleeves at his printing works. Eric was involved in the merchandising for Freddie Starr and when the opportunity for a live Freddie Starr album came up, Eric suggested we start our own label, which became Kamera.

The label's next release after the Freddie Starr album was Roger Chapman's *Mail Order Magic*.

Chris Youle: Downstairs in the Bonaparte packing dept worked a young man called Saul Galpern who started spending more time in my office than packing so Steve sacked him, and he came to work for Kamera. The Au Pairs transferred to Kamera and the label started to look like a typical indie label.

Saul Galpern: Bonaparte was mail-order – it acted almost like Amazon does now – if you wanted the latest hip punk record and you lived in Inverness or wherever, where there were no record shops, you could order them from the back of the *NME*. I started

[55] Record label owned and run by Robert Stigwood, notorious CEO of RSO and Bee Gees manager. He was famously dangled out of a fourth-floor window by Don Arden after attempting to poach the Small Faces from him.
[56] Note Mark's (deliberate?) mixing up of *Saturday Night Fever* and *Grease*.

off putting records into mailers, but I was seeing all these bands every night, so I moved because Chris had a track record of being involved in the record industry and I was new, just coming into it. He was an incredible character to work for. He spent most of his time in the pub, which is probably what Mark went for! But Chris was incredibly bright, very smart. My main memory of that time was Kay shouting and swearing, going mental, but in a good way. That was my induction, seeing a manager who operated on that level. She was really funny too.

Chris Youle: Versa Manos, who I knew from our time at Polydor, needed office space and I suggested to Steve that he let her have the top floor at Bonaparte in return for favourable terms for doing our PR. Versa was already involved with Mark and Kay and it was through this connection that we ended up doing business with them. I was very honest with Mark and Kay – they knew I had very little time for the Sex Pistols, despised The Clash and loathed Rough Trade. But I promised we would get *Hex* into the *Music Week* charts rather than just the *NME* indie chart.

Kay Carroll: I really thought long and hard about leaving The Fall, because my experience [with Rough Trade] felt so disrespectful. The meeting with Kamera came along, added new life and a challenge for me, and allowed us to check out other creative avenues, and so I decided to stay. It became a good opportunity for all parties to make the break, a new beginning. And Mark was gung-ho about it too.

Mark E. Smith: I was very unfamiliar with London at the time, and the bloke who owned the label was always trying to get me out for a drink. A real old-school fucker – he was a good laugh. He took me to Stringfellow's. It was great.

Chris Youle: I would entertain them at Morton's in Berkeley Square and Cristal may have been drunk. They also visited my home and met the family.[57] Somewhere I have a notebook of Mark's that he left behind. Eric and I also visited Mark and Kay at their flat. We enjoyed each other's company and were very fair in our business dealings. We made sure there was a clause which gave them back the rights to the recordings if anything went wrong with the label. I'd like to think Mark enjoyed his time at Kamera because no one gave him any bullshit! I told him our job was to do our best to sell whatever he presented to us in whatever packaging he wanted.

Saul Galpern: Chris would disappear for hours on end, which was how I ended up having to make decisions. It was a good grounding for me to go on and do what I did later on.[58] But I have very fond memories of that time, and Chris in particular.

For Mark, Kamera represented everything he required from a record label. Total artistic control, faith in his instincts and, crucially, enough financial backing to allow him to realise his vision. Now there was only one more adjustment to be made before Mark was ready to record his ultimate Fall album. Something had to be done about the drummer.

---

[57] Quoted in Simon Ford's *Hip Priest*, Kay mistakes Chris's house for Saul Galpern's, but they had most of their dealings with Chris Youle, as confirmed to me by both Chris and Saul.

[58] Saul was later the owner and MD of Nude Records, home of Suede, Billy Mackenzie, Black Box Recorder and many others.

K.K. BURNS BABE –
UMPTEENTH BREAK IN DOWN CURVE

Martin Bramah: That's the Fall I was listening to the most. That period with Marc Riley, Craig Scanlon, Steve and Paul Hanley, Karl Burns … that's my favourite period.

Shortly after our return from Iceland, a band meeting was convened (I wasn't present) where Mark outlined several issues with my recent performances. This included my sub-standard drumming on the recent Peel session, my perpetually hung-over state in Reykjavik and my difficulty in adding appropriate drumming to 'Iceland' – which eventually meant I was pointedly left off the writing credits. Mark certainly had a point about the hangovers, though I was far from alone in suffering the effects of a beer-free regime. His problems with my drumming, on the other hand, mostly boiled down to the fact that I wasn't as good as Karl. In an ideal world he would probably have had Karl replace me, but his grievances weren't fundamental enough to get agreement from everyone else. What had become apparent following the European and US tours was that everyone, including me, liked having Karl around. For Mark's part he acted as a useful buffer and, when required, a double agent between the group's two power bases. For the rest of us he was an absolutely hilarious presence who seemed to make every situation more exciting, for good or ill. The solution Mark came up with was certainly unusual, but it made sense. The group would continue as a six-piece, with two drummers, and I could either shape up or ship out.[59]

Steve Hanley: We'd have a rehearsal with Karl and I'm sure Karl would go back and tell Mark everything that was said.

[59] The Glitter Band and Showaddywaddy both had two drummers, as did The Grateful Dead on occasion. Adam & The Ants had recently built their new sound entirely around a double drum line-up.

Marc Riley: Karl was always Mark's ally. He'd always throw a spanner in the works. He was very crafty, but Mark liked that. Mark's plan was to undermine the little powerbase of us four, who he referred to as the South Manchester lot, though Craig was from Chadderton. But he was a great drummer, and quite entertaining to have around.

Once Mark had decided this, he left Karl and me to figure out exactly how to make it work. One important thing in our favour was that Karl's style had become significantly less flamboyant since his first tenure. Though this was primarily necessitated by having to play my (and to a lesser extent Mike's) drum patterns, it was also true that the role had changed a little. On *Witch Trials* Karl had played pretty much whatever he wanted, but now everything was subject to Mark's approval. And while this change might or might not have made Karl a better drummer, depending on your point of view, it certainly made it easier for the two of us to play together. Which was just as well, as we had just under two weeks before our next gig. The full *Hex Enduction Hour* line-up made its debut at Fagin's, Manchester, on 30th September 1981.

Of the unrecorded songs we already had, 'Fantastic Life', 'Fortress' and 'Deer Park' were immediately converted to fit dual drums, while others saw one of us reluctantly relegated to tambourine. Karl was charged with operating Mark's tape recorder (and later playing second bass), and for the rest of the numbers I was assigned to whatever Marc wasn't playing, e.g. guitar on 'Winter' and keyboards on 'Session Musician'. This new arrangement certainly achieved Mark's aim of keeping us on our toes, both metaphorically and literally. In fact he was forced to acknowledge as much at one of the new line-up's early gigs:

Mark E. Smith: As you can see, ladies and gentlemen, we've decided to improve the visual interest of the group, so if you keep your eyes open you can see people walking around profusely.[60]

[60] This was three gigs into the new six-piece line-up, and when writing out the sets Mark was making no allowances for who played what on which songs. Hence the set included the following sequence: 'Session Musician' (Karl on drums, me on keyboards)/

The one song we had that seemed tailor-made for two drummers, 'Lie Dream of a Casino Soul', was somewhat inevitably deemed out-of-bounds by Mark, given to Karl, and promptly ear-marked as our next single. It was difficult not to see this as a snub, given that I'd come up with the drum part, but I did have to admit it sounded amazing when Karl played it.

'Look, Know' (both on drums)/ 'Who Makes the Nazis?' (me on drums, Karl playing a cassette through Craig's vocal mic)/ 'How I Wrote Elastic Man' (both on drums)/ 'Winter' (Karl on drums, me on guitar). Some of the stages we were playing on at that time weren't really big enough for two drum kits, so clambering in and out was often a challenge. It must have looked ridiculous.

'GINGR' – ProduceR – Smuggler

The new six-piece line-up were hurriedly booked into a London studio with a new producer. Perhaps surprisingly, given the wonderful job he'd done on 'Hip Priest' and 'Iceland', Grant wasn't afforded the opportunity to continue expanding the group's sound. But buoyed by the move to a new and financially generous label, Mark was keen to explore new production avenues.

Richard Mazda: I was the singer and guitarist in a band called Tours, we were a real favourite of John Peel's – he played 'Language School' for fifty nights running. We eventually signed for Virgin. I kind of fell into the role of Tours' producer as well because I was the only person willing to organise things. I'd watch the engineers and by learning on the job I was able to bridge the gap between engineers and out of control musicians! You could either say I was a chancer or a really quick learner – the truth is probably somewhere in the middle.

Virgin wanted us to use Rockpile's rhythm section instead of our own, and Ronnie Mayor, our other singer, split the band rather than deal with them. So I started a new band, The Cosmetics, and eventually Miles Copeland offered me a record deal. I didn't take it – I thought the money was too low – that's how arrogant I was in those days! But Miles was impressed with the demo's production, especially when he heard we'd done it for a hundred quid – so he had me listen to a couple of the bands he'd signed to I.R.S. to see what I thought of the production. One of the bands was The Fleshtones, a great garage band, and my main feeling was 'where's the party?' because I knew what a garage band like that should sound like. I got a call from Miles the next day and a week later I was in RKO Studios in Bloomsbury with everybody looking at me to tell them what to do. We got an outrageously out of control sound on 'The World Has Changed' – it was like a steamroller coming at you.

After that, Miles arranged a meeting with Mark and Kay. Mark asked me what I thought I could do for The Fall. He said he was frustrated that the roar of the band wasn't being captured on record. I told him I'd loved 'Totally Wired' and 'Muzorewi's Daughter' but they sounded like they were played through a transistor radio – there was no bottom end. He thought the way I thought about sound was interesting, so he asked me to produce a single.

Grant Showbiz: Richard Mazda was a strange choice but then so was I in a way, with *Dragnet*. [But] I was up to my neck in post-punk indie at Street-Level – before 'indie' became a byword for 'twee'. To be honest *Room To Live* was a bit tougher as I'd been involved so much up till then ... but of course I returned![61]

Richard Mazda: Mark left it to me to choose the studio, so I suggested The Workhouse – it was Manfred Mann's studio but half the time they rented it out for sessions. Its set-up was basically a copy of Townhouse studios[62] – they had a stone room, where you could get an amazing drum sound, and a seventies 'dead' room, so it was perfect for two drummers. I was flying by the seat of my pants – I don't think I'd even heard a demo of 'Lie Dream' before we went in. I put Karl in the stone room and when we were finally ready to hit record I was astounded by the sheer power of the band.

'Lie Dream of a Casino Soul' was first played live in February 1981, though the musical arrangement and lyric were both still fairly sketchy at that point. Mark had also used the gist of the title ('this next track mistreats the lie of the Wigan soul dream') to introduce a different song as early as January. On the single's sleeve Mark ties the song to *Hex*'s main character: 'This is the pre-amble youthful ramble of Big Priest.'

[61] I think Grant had every right to be a bit put-out at not getting to produce all of *Hex*, given what a fantastic job he did on 'Hip Priest' and 'Iceland', but he's far too nice a guy to complain.
[62] Townhouse, in Shepherd's Bush, was owned by Richard Branson and in the eighties was the go-to studio for bands that wanted a 'big sound'. Its stone room was utilised to striking effect on Phil Collins's 'In The Air Tonight'.

The lyric tells the story of a northern soul aficionado who spends his weekends at Wigan Casino all-nighters, fuelled by pills which suppress his hunger and cause strange hallucinations. He is scornful of all other types of music, particularly the Kraftwerk albums his brother has brought back from working in Germany. 'I think I'll cut my dick off, the trouble it got me in' was, according to Mark at the time, a more-or-less verbatim quote from someone he knew who was a Wigan Casino regular.[63]

Mark's attitude to Wigan Casino in particular and to northern soul boys in general was mostly affectionate. Mainly though, Mark was conscious that their inherent distrust of anything mainstream had left them high and dry when the new wave of post-*Quadrophenia* mod groups, and Dexys Midnight Runners in particular, co-opted the sounds they loved.[64] Of course, as with most of his pronouncements, his opinion was flexible depending on who he was talking to.[65]

He noted, with some regret, that the Wigan soul boys hadn't moved on to other types of music:

Mark E. Smith: A lot of those kids who went to the Wigan Casino … this is what 'Lie Dream Of The Casino Soul' is about, y'know those kids are not interested in rock at all, it's fuckin' tragic. Young, healthy kids … I mean, that's why record sales are going down, coz it's a lot of shit, man, and of course these kids think of The Fall as the same as all these other pretentious groups.

He later expressed regret that 'Lie Dream' had been interpreted as an overt criticism of the northern soul boys themselves:

[63] It is written as 'Mein Dyckhoff' on the sleeve to avoid a potential radio ban. Dyckhoff was a German department store and Mark had been using one of their carrier bags as his briefcase since the last European tour.

[64] Based on The Who's brilliant 1973 album of the same name, *Quadrophenia* (the film) was released in September 1979 and seemed to spawn a brand-new wave of mini-mods overnight. As a 15-year-old schoolboy and inveterate musical snob, I was particularly scornful when all the kids who were too self-conscious to get into punk/new wave suddenly started turning up in khaki parkas and professing a life-long love of Booker T. & the M.G.'s. Of course, The Jam were the bridge between the two musical schools and were consequently massive at the time.

[65] Mark said he wanted the music for 'Lie Dream of a Casino Soul' to be 'a bit 'mod'. As a consequence the drum beat is 'influenced' by Secret Affair's 'Let Your Heart Dance'.

Mark E. Smith: That song actually did create quite a bit of resentment in the north because people thought it was being snobby and horrible about the old soul boys, which it was never about anyway. Because I was brought up with people that were into northern soul five years before anybody down here [London] had even heard about it. But they've all grown out of it, which is what the song is about, but it wasn't putting them down at all. If anything, it was glorifying them, but not in the format of, where are those soul boys that used to be here? There are actually a lot of old soul boys who like The Fall, because that music was always offbeat and it gives them a feeling for the sort of wackiness that you find in our music. It's really funny because Dexys bust a gut trying to attract that audience and never even got close. All the kids I know just thought it was pathetic 'cause they were wearing the clothes they'd been wearing six years ago and ripping off all these horn riffs that they knew off by heart from the originals.

Musically, the single version was much tighter and more precise than the version recorded for John Peel a year earlier, and it was an obvious choice for a single, despite the lack of a discernible chorus. It also boasted a breakdown section in the middle which highlighted both Marc's neat keyboard riff and Karl's mastery of the explosive re-entry. Though there are numerous occasions where it could be argued that the Peel versions of songs capture something that is missing from the official release, 'Lie Dream' was not one of them. The production, arrangement and performance were all head and shoulders above the version recorded at Maida Vale.[66]

Craig Scanlon: I think the reason a lot of people prefer the Peel versions is because they were always done with different producers who wouldn't put up with being shouted down the ear by Mark. People like Buffin, who was a brilliant producer.[67] He knew what Mark was like and he'd say 'you go to the pub' and do all his stuff while Mark wasn't there.

[66] Especially the hand-claps. The hand-claps were brilliant.
[67] Aka Dale Griffin, erstwhile drummer for Mott The Hoople. Hated being reminded of his former career for some unfathomable reason.

As he had been brought in as a 'name' producer, Richard had a bit more authority than The Fall's previous producers. Like the BBC soundmen, he was less susceptible to Mark's hectoring.

Marc Riley: Richard Mazda made a real difference to the sound. I think Mark made a conscious decision to make the record more palatable. He was ambitious. Sometimes he wanted to be in the charts and make money. He didn't want to be underground all the time.

Richard Mazda: We captured something that they hadn't had before, real bottom end in the bass, and the drums hitting you in the chest. 'Lie Dream' was an amazing single.

The B-side, 'Fantastic Life', was the first time the full two-drummer line-up was heard on record, and it was this track that convinced everyone that an album with two drummers would work. For a start, Karl and I figured out how to play together in a way which complemented each other rather than clashed. The secret was for one drummer to play the bass drum part and act as a human click-track while the other sat on top.[68]

Richard Mazda: The studio at Workhouse had sight lines that meant at minimum both drummers could see each other.

This electrifying new era in The Fall's history is ushered in by a four-handed flam as the song begins, and the exhilaration all of us felt knowing we'd pulled it off is tangible, you can even hear it in Mark's unusually animated delivery. What's more the song loops through several more A–B sections than the lyric requires, as if no one wants it to end.

---

[68] It sounds easier than it was. Though drummers nowadays are used to playing along with a click, in those days having something/someone else dictating the tempo was most unusual.

Marc Riley: The two-drummer thing was a great thing to do. You felt like you couldn't fail with that going on behind you. And with Steve it was a great base for a band. It was impenetrable, a force of nature.

Craig Scanlon: Live 'Fantastic Life' was proper, manic VU stuff. It would go on forever.

The lyric is particularly enjoyable – it's one of Mark's least preoccupied texts and, as with 'New Face in Hell', the self-imposed limit in subject matter allows for a more playful and nuanced use of language, and 'fantastic' is used to mean both 'fanciful' and 'superb' throughout the song.

Mark has often talked of his fondness for 'daft history books' and on 'Fantastic Life' we're able to witness first-hand his pleasure in reading outlandish conspiracy theories.[69] He derived similar joy from listening to the self-aggrandising raconteurs he often encountered in pubs, and it's his reaction to both kinds of 'fantastic lie' which makes this song so satisfying.

At one point Mark outlines the obviously bonkers theory that the role of magic mushrooms in the creation of the Santa Claus myth is somehow linked to Rasputin's exposing of Jack the Ripper as a Russian doctor.

Steve Hanley: 'The Siberian mushroom Santa was in fact Rasputin's brother' is the greatest line of all time!

We also meet a former spy who now enjoys liquid breakfasts, and a binman who boasts of his previous life as a Palestinian agent provocateur in 1948. Mark also throws in references to China's over-reliance on antibiotics and governmental interference in the Royal Mail for good measure. The final – and by implication no

[69] In the song 'Hotel Blöedel' he outlines a well-known and wonderfully crackers conspiracy theory about two thousand dead Tibetan monks found in Berlin in 1945 dressed in SS uniforms. His admission of his fondness for 'daft history books' comes from an interview with *Vulture* where he discusses reading similarly far-fetched stories about the Hittites.

less fantastic – tale we're treated to is Dave Tucker's account of how he stood up to a copper on Corporation Street, which of course Mark doesn't believe a word of.[70]

Fall songs that are so resolutely upbeat in both lyric and music are rare, and coupled with the band's audible excitement at the potential of this new line-up, it makes for exhilarating listening.

Equally exciting was the production, which managed to capture the two drummers while still highlighting the guitar, keys and bass. Mark attributed enough of the track's success to Richard Mazda to retain his services for what would become *Hex Enduction Hour*. Given the importance Mark had placed on the new album, this was praise indeed.

---

[70] Dave played on and off with the band during 1981, he did backing vocals on *Slates* and played clarinet on the Peel version of 'Lie Dream'. Once Karl resumed his role as Mark's sounding-board Dave was surplus to requirements. Nice guy, but I'm not having he gave the policeman what-for either.

SUITS OFF, JEANS ON

The recording session that made up the bulk of the album took place at The Regal in Hitchin.

Later reviews and references to the album usually give the impression that the group broke into a derelict building and recorded on mobile equipment in order to ensure that our rejection of studio artifice was created with sufficient vérité.

> Recorded in such disparate locales as a lava-walled studio in Iceland and an abandoned theatre in a town on the outskirts of Luton, England. – *Pop Matters*

> In typically obtuse fashion, other tracks were recorded in an empty cinema in Hitchin. – *Record Collector*

> The band recorded the remainder of the album in a movie theatre that was going unused. – *Diffuser*

Mark himself hasn't been averse to playing up to this mythos either:

Mark E. Smith: We had two drummers and studios were changing at the time because everyone was getting into synth music so I thought we should go to an old cinema and get a bit of a live feel to it. And Kamera just went right along with it. They were good like that. So we recorded part of it in a cave and part of it in a cinema.

But this wasn't in any way the case, nor was it an example of Mark's idiosyncrasy or recalcitrance. In truth, The Regal was neither empty nor abandoned, and recording there was a highly logical choice. In 1981, The Regal was a thriving concert venue which also housed a bespoke 16-track recording studio located on the upper floor.[71] Unusually, the venue was also wired for recording directly from the stage – because of this it was used for several BBC 'In-Concerts' by the likes of The Fun Boy Three, Squeeze, 10cc and Thin Lizzy. All of which meant it perfectly suited a group with two drummers that wanted to capture the best elements of their live sound and still leave room for studio recording and enhancement where necessary. Which is why Richard Mazda suggested it.

Richard Mazda: The Workhouse wasn't available, so Hitchin was my idea. One reason was that although it was in a town it was almost like getting away to the country to record, because Hitchin had no music scene of its own. But the real reason we went there was because of its capacity to record on the stage. We recorded it basically very live. This was to try and catch the incredible energy of how they played live and frankly because it wouldn't have worked to record The Fall by layers, recording individual parts. The lack of separation wasn't an issue – one can argue that having the sounds co-mingling is how the band and audience experienced the music anyway, and I was a big believer in maintaining the energy that bands felt when rehearsing or playing live. Even at The Workhouse everyone except Karl was in one room.

In many ways this was a conscious rejection of the prevailing wisdom. It was, for instance, the exact opposite approach to the one used to incredible effect by Martin Hannett in his ground-breaking production for Joy Division. For Hannett, separation was key. For the initial *Hex Enduction Hour* tracks, it wasn't merely unimportant, it was impossible.

The band set up on stage, albeit differently to our normal stage configuration. The two drum kits were set up facing towards each other, so each of us could see what the other was doing. The amps were pointed away from the drums to reduce bleeding, and the three musicians stood in a circle. It was impossible to capture a

[71] The Regal began life in 1939 as a 1055-seater cinema. Like many of the massive pre-war cinemas it struggled in the seventies and ran its final film – *Secrets of a Super Stud* (which featured Throbbing Gristle's Cosey Fanni Tutti in a minor role) in December 1977. It was extensively refurbished and reopened as recording studio and concert hall in July 1980.

clean vocal from Mark with the band on stage, so he was billeted in the recording facility upstairs. He could just about see us – the studio was in the old projection room and had a large window – but we couldn't really see him. All we had was his disembodied voice in our headphones. This wasn't as unusual as it might sound, as baffles and separators often block sight lines when you're recording, but having Mark so far away definitely added to the ever present him-and-us dynamic.

Craig Scanlon: I didn't like it. It wasn't a studio, we played on the stage. I understand the concept of it, because we were a very good live band, but I think it's a thin sound. I think it was better in the upstairs studio.

Despite the prevailing legend, less than half the album was recorded on the stage, and the whole band moved into the upstairs studio halfway through the session. The main reason for this was the acceptance that certain tracks were better suited to a more traditional studio environment. But there was a more practical motive too, at least for some of us. There's some debate as to the exact date the recording took place, but it was definitely in the middle of the harshest weather conditions any of us had ever experienced. In fact December 1981 and January 1982 saw some of the coldest, snowiest and severest winter weather ever recorded in the UK.

Marc Riley: It was this cavernous place with no heating. Absolutely freezing.

Steve Hanley: Mark, of course, was upstairs in the nice warm studio. 'The lads don't need heating.' So as we were staying in a pub ten minutes up the road, the big thing was to try and get it wrapped up and make it back to the pub for last orders at half ten.

Craig Scanlon: We usually only made it to the pub because Mark wasn't a big fan of us all sitting round listening to him trying to do his vocals.

[SIDE ONE: TRACK 1] **The Classical**

Words: Smith **Music:** Burns-Hanley (S)-Hanley (P)-Riley-Scanlon-Smith

(Smith/The Fall)

Smith vocal, keyboards; *Riley* guitar; *Scanlon* guitar, vocal; *Hanley (S)* bass; *Burns* drums; *Hanley (P)* drums

First played live: 7th December 1981, The Venue, London

Recorded: December 1981, stage, Regal Cinema, Hitchin[72]

Producer: Richard Mazda. **Engineer:** Tony J. Sutcliffe

Released: 8th March 1982

---

[72] *The Big Midweek* dates the Hitchin sessions to January 1982, but this would have meant that the turnaround between recording and release was less than two months, which seems unrealistically efficient for both The Fall and Kamera.

Keep Shtum

Once the tape was rolling everyone forgot about the cold. As on many of *Hex*'s 'stage' songs, the band's sense of excitement is palpable on 'The Classical'. This is particularly true of Karl and me, as we were delighted with our respective drum parts and the way they complimented each other.[73]

Most of the songs on *Hex* were written when the group had only one drummer, and either remained that way ('Hip Priest', 'Winter', 'Who Makes The Nazis?', 'Iceland') or were adapted for two ('Fortress/Deer Park'; 'Jawbone and the Air-Rifle') and as such could have easily been adapted back if the two drummers idea hadn't worked, which was a real possibility. 'The Classical' is one of the best examples of a Fall song where two drummers are central and it doesn't really work with only one. It was worked up at the group's office/rehearsal space at 429b Bury New Road.

Steve Hanley: It's different booking a rehearsal room you're paying for by the hour and having a rehearsal place where you can go at any time. That's what made the difference on that album.

In fact the group probably spent more 'down time' together during this period than at any time since Martin, Una and Tony were on board.[74] It also changed the dynamic of the songwriting process, as for the first time songs were worked out with drums

---

[73] It was also thrilling to have someone really listening to what you were doing – let's face it, while they're playing, guitarists and singers only ever notice when the drummer does something wrong.

[74] Obviously much of this time was spent finding excuses not to play. The House That Jack Built, a bizarre pub purpose-built to suit its name, was probably the biggest beneficiary of our various work-avoidance schemes. There was also a memorable foray to Mandley Park for a kickabout, which was abandoned before a ball was played after Mark insisted on measuring out a huge pitch with full-sized goalmouths for a game of three-a-side. After much debate Mark announced, 'Well if you want to play a kids' game,' and proved he was much more adult by flouncing off with the ball.

from the beginning, rather than added on as an afterthought. This difference in approach had a profound effect on 'The Classical' in particular. For once everyone was pitching in, though understandably after 37 years no one can agree who went first.

Marc Riley: I think we had the drums first, and I had this weird riff, which wasn't chords, it was just barring. That's how it started. I could play it for you now, and it still sounds odd. Craig's thing came after. When it came to adding Craig's part it wasn't like 'play an A' or anything it was 'just try something'.

Craig Scanlon: I wrote 'The Classical' – I was dead proud of it – was basically conducting the lot of you in a rehearsal.[75] I told you to keep the beat and be Ringo, and Karl to be the heavy metal monster and do the fills. I only gave Marc the 'never felt better in my life' tune, and he wasn't going to just stand there for five minutes, so he made up his own discordant thing.

Steve Hanley: Craig didn't write it all – he certainly didn't write the bass solo at the end. John Taylor wrote that for 'Planet Earth'.

The traditional beat (played by me) is contrasted and enhanced by Karl's manic percussion part, played for the most part on his snare with the snares off. Performing the same role as congas traditionally do in a samba, Karl's percussion transports the song from traditional indie territory into something far more ear-catching and plays tricks with the listener's perception of how fast or slow the song is. As Mark later confirmed, this temporal misdirection was a key aspect of the whole album:

Mark E. Smith: That's the good thing about *Hex*, I was experimenting with speeding up on a track and slowing down, trying to get the group to play out of time. It's weird because I never sing in time. The last thing you want is regular time.

---

[75] As Craig's quotes are taken from a personal interview the 'you' here is me. As we don't get to hear his voice nearly enough these days I've reproduced Craig's words verbatim.

Much of 'The Classical's musical fascination comes from the fact that for most of the song Marc's guitar and the rhythm and bass are playing in two different keys, as folk singer Stuart Estell has pointed out, though he was a little out on the details of who was playing what.[76]

Stuart Estell: The problem for 'normal' ears is that 'The Classical' is, in muso-speak, bi-tonal – in two keys at once. The bass part is in a mode of A, while Scanlon's scratchy guitar part is in something like C#. That's why the sound of the thing changes so much when it gets to 'I've never felt better...' – at that point Scanlon's chords start following the bass part and suddenly everyone's playing in the same key.

Craig Scanlon: I'm in two minds about it. It could have been a bit more melodic, but everybody loves 'The Classical' because of that discord. It does work. You have to trust the people you've got, and we had a really good team there. And live we made it better and better – when everybody went at the same time it was a real hairs on the back of your neck moment. 'I've never felt better in my life' – that's beautiful.

As a means of reflecting Mark's lyric, the jump from an unsettling bi-tonal discord into a harmonious resolve has rarely been bettered, and the moment, as well as the song itself, was lauded by journalist Nathaniel Friedman in *Billboard* magazine, no less, as one of the group's finest:

> There's no definitive Fall song. But if you had to pick one, you could do far worse than 'The Classical'. ... The opening riff, all rumbling guitar, bass, and drums, is a fanfare for a track that, as it turns out, never really exists. Almost as soon as it starts, 'The Classical' begins falling apart – toying with decay, fraying around the edges, plunging the listener into uncertainty even as it surges

---

[76] Estell probably has the shortest tenure of anyone who can claim to have played with The Fall – he played guitar for one song, from the audience, at a gig at Reading Alleycat on 30th April 1998.

forward. The rhythm section vamps ominously and shards of guitar splinter the air. It sounds like all hell is about to break loose. ... But the breakthrough, however fleeting, is exultant. 'The Classical' builds to Smith groaning 'I've never felt better in my life' over an unusually melodic riff. He knows how stupid it sounds and this makes him giddy; it's not the triumph of the absurd, it's the absurdity of triumph – of pulling something off that probably should have killed you.

In fact, 'The Classical' is one of the best examples of the early Fall's ability to use their non-musicianship to their advantage. What music lecturer and Manchester musician Richard Witts calls 'the dissonance achieved through three means – tuning, bitonality and looseness of co-ordination' is, of course, entirely instinctive, though no less effective for that.[77]

> The understandable tendency for reviewers to focus on Mark's lyrics unduly subordinates the sound world in which they're set, and discounts the musicians who contribute so much to the fabric of the experience. ... Those songs were not so much constructed as discovered, realised by the members working out through time random ideas.

The unmusicality of 'The Classical' was later thrown into sharp relief when an attempt was made to score the song for the Royal Scottish Orchestra. Ballet dancer and choreographer Michael Clark, who worked with The Fall many times, wanted to use it for his ballet *Hail the Classical*. Simon Rogers, who later became a member of The Fall himself, was charged with the task, but it never came to fruition. Mark was convinced the fault lay with the musicians.

Mark E. Smith: You're talking about two chords and about three inflections in the whole song.[78] Simon scored the whole

---

[77] Dick Witts was a member of Tony Friel's immediate post-Fall group The Passage. He also introduced Mark to Michael Clark.

[78] Though 'The Classical' is hardly Weather Report, Mark deliberately underestimates the number of chords and inflections (i.e. the amount of sophistication therein) to make his point. Why let the truth...

thing for the orchestra and they couldn't get it, they couldn't play the fucker. I mean can you believe it? It's disgusting. You know, it cost a lot of money to score it for a thirty-two-piece orchestra. And I did a vocal tape that they were supposed to play along with. And they couldn't carry it. I couldn't believe it, they couldn't carry it, they couldn't play. It was too difficult.

But of course, the difficulty in navigating 'The Classical's wayward modulation wasn't due to a lack of musical proficiency. The Royal Scottish Orchestra, like any orchestra worth its salt, would have had no problem playing anything at all they were instructed to. It was the act of finding order in the chaos that proved impossible.

Simon Rogers: It was a hopeless task in retrospect and at that time I don't think technically I was up to making a really good orchestral version.

Lyrically, 'The Classical', with the possible exception of 'Hip Priest', is probably *Hex Enduction Hour*'s central track.

Mark E. Smith: 'The Classical' is the song that sums up the fuck-you-very-much attitude best. It's the anthem of the record. I figured: if you want to say it, you might as well do it in the first song.

In some ways 'The Classical' acts as an overture for the rest of the album. Musically, it's loud-then-quiet passages and the way it contrasts between discord and melody sets the group's stall out perfectly. Lyrically it foreshadows many of the preoccupations to come ('Message for yer!') – from bullish self-regard and contempt for others ('Hey there fuck face') to self-doubt and finally acceptance ('I've never felt better in my life').

Certainly, for anyone wishing to get to the heart of Mark E. Smith's lyrical preoccupations, it's a key text and, not at all coincidentally, is markedly contentious. There is, of course, the perennial problem of whether the song is expressing Mark's views, or the narrator is a character. Either way, we're on *extremely* dodgy ground before we get to the end of the first verse.

As opening lines go, 'There is no culture' is quite the opening salvo, and to make matters worse Mark is bragging about it – 'is my brag' – though *The Quietus* founder John Doran suggests this may be a sideswipe at Melvyn Bragg.

John Doran: He was the host of the *South Bank Show* at the time. I get the feeling this is the kind of show ... that really got on Smith's nerves.

Certainly, TV was on Mark's mind, as the sleeve notes for this song make clear:

> Spite does not enter into this. But R. Castle in his useless goals h.q. shadowed by Parachute suite style youths, plus the canned response to C. James (recent tv) Cast a diff. hue to this tune.[79]

There follows the most controversial, and hence most discussed, line in the whole of Mark's prodigious canon.[80] Perhaps the most surprising thing about Mark's use of the N* word to highlight the tokenism of the industry he found himself working in, was how little criticism he received at the time. Of course, the word was not quite as self-evidently inadmissible in 1981 as it would be now. A mere two years previously Elvis Costello had included the word in his biggest hit single, 'Oliver's Army', which reached number two in the charts. The song enjoyed massive airplay across

---

[79] 'R. Castle in his useless goals h.q.' is a reference to *Record Breakers*, a BBC TV children's show that ran from 1972 to 2001. Light entertainer Roy Castle was the main presenter, and the show featured various attempts to complete the 'useless goal' of bettering entries in the *Guinness Book of Records*. The *Clive James on TV* show was a sneering look at the worst excesses of foreign TV, mainly built round the mildly racist schadenfreude that we would never be subjected to such trash. Inevitably, many of the ideas, such as *Endurance*'s eating challenges and bizarre physical punishments, were later taken up by British TV shows such as *I'm a Celebrity...Get Me Out of Here!* and proved to be massive ratings hits. As Mark noted in a separate press release, 'T.V. is riddled now with liquefied "satire" in most cases inferior to what the "satirists" are trying to takea da piss out of.'
[80] Though it's got quite a bit of competition.

93

Radio 1 and the commercial networks and was even performed on *Top of the Pops* without censure or even a coy cut away to the bass player while it was being sung. The context of the word in 'Oliver's Army' is possibly less troublesome than the way it's used in 'The Classical', though both are markedly ironic, but clearly two wrongs don't make a right.

Discussing the album, John Doran placed Mark's use of the word firmly in the middle of a continuum of 'hipster' white artists – Dylan, Lennon and Patti Smith as well as Costello. These writers, he argues, used the word in an attempt to highlight their own edgy coolness, all the while remaining uncharacteristically oblivious to the possibility that by using the word they themselves were being racist. Mark himself was utterly convinced that his use of the word was self-evidently not bigoted – to the point that he openly mocked anyone who was offended. When interviewed by Sandy Robertson for *Sounds* shortly after the album was released, he drew attention to a recent review by Marc Storace:

Mark E. Smith: And did you see *Flexipop*, where this Swiss guy from Krokus said … we were racist because I sing 'obligatory n★★★★★s'…[81]

It's worth noting that the asterisks are my own, *Sounds* had no problem with printing the word in full. Robertson's comment on this, 'We laugh. What else can you do in the face of such malign ignorance?' is equally telling. And, while it wouldn't have mattered anyway, it would also be remiss of me not to acknowledge the fact none of the band had much to say about the offending line at the time either.

Marc Riley: At the time I never thought he was being racist, I thought he was being a third person. It wasn't celebrating it. I thought he was having a go at racists.

[81] Krokus were, and still are, a profoundly humourless prog-cum-heavy metal outfit from Switzerland. Their albums include *Pay It In Metal*, *Metal Rendez-vous* and my personal favourite *To Rock or Not to Be*.

Steve Hanley: It is true that none of us said 'I'm not playing that song if you're going to use that word', and I think he would say he was being a character anyway. But you wouldn't get away with it today.

Craig Scanlon: Mark was heavily into Wyndham Lewis and *Blast*, making big statements that are supposed to shock you. It was also a dig at the white middle-class hipsters. I didn't think it was ill meant, but I can't defend it now.

Surprisingly, none of the band was asked to defend the line at the time either, which is just as well, as Mark clarified what he meant in the fanzine *Allied Propaganda* a year later. Needless to say, he remained resolutely, and uncomfortably, unapologetic.

Mark E. Smith: There was stuff like 'obligatory n*****s' and that, which has like come true, and every programme you see about young people has now got a black boy in it. I have to make a joke about that, I can't help it.

But even leaving aside the ad hominem of trying to fathom Mark's real views, it's still surprising that the line wasn't condemned in and for itself, irate Swiss metal singers aside. The likely amount of opprobrium never came. Mark got away with the line all-but scot-free, and it's not immediately obvious why. As Brian Edge pointed out in his 1989 book *Paintwork – A Portrait of The Fall*:

> Why The Fall were never carpeted for the word was a complete mystery. Joy Division, New Order, and Siouxsie and the Banshees were all clapped in irons at one time or another for alleged anti-Semitism. Even The Cure found themselves in hot water for the dubiously-titled "Killing an Arab". ... So how did Mark Smith escape the wrath of the moral arbiters?

John Doran has admitted he was amongst those guilty of swerving the controversy when he first reviewed *Hex* and this track in particular. He originally concluded that the line was 'not racist in the context of the song', though he did admit it was 'unpleasant to say the least'. Perhaps we should be grateful he addressed it at all. Reviews in *NME*, *Sounds* and *Melody Maker* at the time of its release saw no reason to draw attention to the line, though *Melody Maker*'s (by Colin Irwin no less) did at least acknowledge the song's 'hate'.

Mark Fisher's theory is that it was the 'unplaceability of any of the utterances on *Hex* that allowed Smith to escape censure for the notorious line. Intent was unreadable. Everything sounds like a citation, embedded discourse, mention rather than use.' In short, Mark gets away with it because we're never sure why he said it, or at what points in the song (if any) the character singing is himself.

This point has been expanded on by Jim B, a contributor to the 'Fall: Album By Album' discussion board:

> His ability to combine first, second, and third character narratives, often in the same song and sometimes in the same verse, his use of such narrative devices such as the unreliable narrative voice and epistolary narrative voice, his confusing of narrative time (past, present and future), his perversion of the normal rules of syntax and his choice to just use certain words and lines for sonic rather than narrative effect. He is also extremely sarcastic. Combine all those things, sometimes all in one song, and it seems a little meaningless to pull out words at random for scrutiny when only MES really knows why they are there.

It's worth pointing out though that when The Fall resurrected the song in 2002 the offending line was left out. Perhaps twenty years on even Mark E. Smith could grow tired of defending the indefensible.

Elsewhere, and somewhat less controversially, there's room for Mark's theory that 'there are twelve people in the world, the rest are paste'. Like his theory on 'Underground Medecin', which is alluded to in both 'Rowche Rumble' and 'Fit and Working again',[82] the 'paste' theory was one of Mark's go-to theories

---

[82] 'Kick your liver in, treat it like the bin' and 'gimme gimme U.G. medecin' respectively.

which often popped up in other songs. Paste, in this context, is the substance that costume jewellery is made of, and as 'paste' was sometimes replaced by 'slate' live, this ties the sentiment in with the lyric of 'Slates, Slags, Etc.' that the world is full of imitators of the truly talented.[83] The proliferation of 'plagiarisation and blackboard type people in this land of ours' was a particular bugbear of Mark's, and those content to be pale imitations always came in for particular criticism. This was especially true for those who imitated The Fall,[84] as he pointed out in 'Hip Priest':

> All the young groups know they can imitate but I teach, because I'm a Hip Priest.

The lyric also expresses his disgust with the design of Wilkinson-Sword's 'Profile' disposable razor, adverts for which were all over the TV at the time. Over several live performances this section of the song evolved into a similar rant about the design flaws of a fictional new car, the Ford/Kawasaki Excel Escort. Though it was a little contrived – Mark had far less personal grievance with poorly designed cars than with razors that weren't fit for purpose[85] – the shortcomings of the car's ability to cope with weather extremes did allow for a nice segue back into the main part of the song via a lovely pun on the word 'hail'.

Unusually for Mark, he was proud to call 'The Classical' an anthem – he normally avoided such 'this is me' pronunciations at all costs. It may even have been a ploy to deflect attention from the self-revelation that was more obviously inherent on tracks like 'Hip Priest'. 'The Classical' he insisted, was 'the only anthem in there'.

One oft-quoted piece of folklore is that 'The Classical', or more specifically a certain line in the song, directly resulted in

---

[83] See also Brix Smith Start's comments at the 2018 *NME* awards: 'Mark told me he believed there were only seven original people in the world, and that everyone else was a slate of one of them.'

[84] 'Notebooks out, plagiarists' was the subtitle of side two of 1991's *Shift-Work*.

[85] Mark never passed his driving test, but up until his later illness he was resolutely clean-shaven and had little time for those who weren't. As evidenced by the lyric to 'How I Wrote Elastic Man', growing a beard was a sure sign you'd let yourself go. During a particularly fractious time on tour in Australia (see *The Big Midweek* for details) we all stopped shaving mainly because we knew it would really piss him off.

The Fall losing a lucrative contract with Motown records. This version of the story, from the *We Are Cult* website, is typical of how it's usually recounted.

> It was 1982 and Motown's UK wing had hired a new A&R man to shake up their rather stale roster. As it happened, the new guy was a big Fall fan. Just the band to shake things up a little, he reasoned. So he convened a boardroom meeting of Motown bigwigs who were eager to hear what all the fuss was about. The A&R guy stuck *Hex Enduction Hour* on the deck and sat back, confident of a positive outcome. 'The Classical' boomed out of the speakers, with Smith yawping, 'Where are the obligatory n*****s? Hey there, fuckface!' The Motown memo apparently read, 'We have listened to The Fall. In our opinion, they have zero commercial potential.' And so it came to pass that Mark E. Smith narrowly failed to become a label stablemate of Smokey Robinson and Marvin Gaye.

The original source of the story was a 1984 interview with Mark himself:

Mark E. Smith: The funny thing was this guy at Motown asked for some of our old stuff he could listen to and the only thing I had was *Hex Enduction Hour* and the first line on that is 'Where are the obligatory n*****s?' I thought, 'When they hear that, we've had it.'

But it's a tale that loses nothing in the telling – a signing-on fee of £46,000 has been attached to the story on some occasions, and by 1994 Mark was adamant that Motown had entered into a legally binding contract:

Mark E. Smith: It was all signed, sealed and delivered, I could have actually got them for millions. I just didn't want to put the guys in London in the shit.

But the truth is slightly more prosaic, as Mick Middles has made clear:

I don't wish to be pedantic, especially if it spoils a good story, but the 'Fall sign to Motown' story has been rather overblown. The label was, in truth, Motown UK, little more than a holding company for its American owner and The Fall interest lay rather more in the fact that it was manned by drifters from the British A&R brat pack – all of whom were big Fall fans – rather than some heartfelt desire on the part of Motown boss Berry Gordy to sign the band.

This version of events is backed up by Richard Thomas, who was managing the group at the time of the potential Motown liaison.

Richard Thomas: Motown were opening up in this country and they were trying to get different people on. It was a very young guy called Alan who was very low down. I met him a couple of times. Mark and Brix met him, and *Hex* was sent to them, but to be honest I don't think it ever would have happened anyway – the Beggars Banquet thing was happening at the same time.

Steve Hanley: I think that's one of Mark's interview stories. He was so good at the press thing, because journalists struggle to get stories out of bands. With Mark you just put the tape on and it was job done.

[SIDE TWO: TRACK 5] **And This Day**

Words: Smith **Music:** Burns-Hanley (S)-Hanley (P)-Riley-Scanlon (Smith/The Fall)

Smith vocal; *Riley* keyboards; *Scanlon* guitar, vocal; *Hanley (S)* bass; *Burns* drums; *Hanley (P)* drums

First played live: 12th March 1982, Bristol Polytechnic

Recorded: December 1981, stage, Regal Cinema, Hitchin

Producer: Richard Mazda. **Engineer:** Tony J. Sutcliffe

Released: 8th March 1982

load o bloody nowt

'And This Day' remains one of the most brutal and uncompromising Fall numbers, as well as one of the longest.[86] Vaguely indebted to the Velvet Underground, it was built around Marc's keyboard riff and a drumbeat, devised at a soundcheck by Karl and me, which is really a riff in its own right. Unlike other such improvised songs ('Hip Priest', 'The Classical') that gradually gained a degree of structure and dynamics over time, 'And This Day' didn't evolve much at all. Everyone just did their own thing, and it shows – the guitar, keyboards and bass are markedly disjointed and only sporadically manage an approximation of the same key. On the record, as live, it holds the ear by dint of its sheer relentless impact alone. Which, given that the performance as recorded lasted 25 minutes, is really quite impressive. The five of us on stage had no idea how long the song would last, we'd only played it a couple of times before and were literally making it up as we went along. We couldn't even see Mark, so we had no idea if he'd finished singing or had another five verses up his sleeve, so we kept on playing, battering the single riff like our life depended on it. Each of us was determined not to be the first to give up. 'No fucking respite', to quote from a lyric that is about as impenetrable as Mark ever got, which is saying something.

Mark E. Smith: 'And This Day', the thing that finishes off the LP and often finishes off a lot of audiences, you know. Like everything's going great until we do 'And This Day' and everyone's going like, STOP, please. So I think that's worthwhile.

[86] The version recorded live at the Hammersmith Palais on 25th March 1982, and later issued on *Hip Priest and Kamerads*, is not for the fainthearted. That version featured Mark and Kay's friend Alan Pillay, and weighed in at an impressive fifteen minutes. Al/Lana Pillay was a long-term friend of Mark and Kay who supported The Fall on numerous occasions and appeared in Mark's play *Hey! Luciani*. She also makes a memorable appearance in the *Perverted By Language/Bis* video reading a poem of Mark's regarding Kim Wilde's gig-going habits, the Stray Cats and the merits of serving cod with tinned tomatoes.

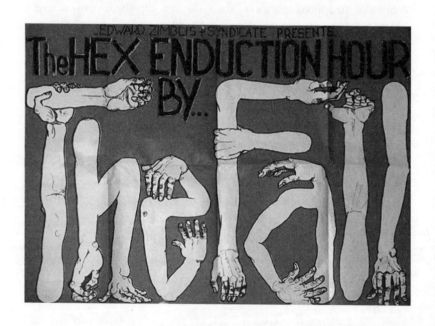

Craig Scanlon: You'd be like 'when's this going to fucking end?' - it was an instrument to pummel the audience with. I think it would have been brilliant with just the drums, Marc on the keyboards and left it at that. I wasn't happy with what I was doing on it. I'd have gladly sat it out.

Marc Riley: 'And This Day' is one of the greatest things we ever did, I think. It wasn't as good a song as say 'Totally Wired', but it was like World War Three! When we played with The Birthday Party, who I think were one of the greatest bands ever, they went on and they threw fire eaters, everything at us just to say 'we're better than The Fall'. It was a real Jerry Lewis 'follow that' moment, and we did. We said we're gonna play these four notes for quarter of an hour, and you can kiss my arse, you'll never get anywhere near that.[87] They threw the gauntlet down and we picked it up and battered them with it. I know there will be Birthday Party fans who'll say 'I was there, The Birthday Party were better', but I'd be the first to say when we did a shit gig, we did loads of them! But that, and the Anti Club in LA, were my two favourite Fall gigs ever.

Steve Hanley: It was weird, and it doesn't seem to happen with bands now, but you could play the same thing, same notes, and one night it would be shit and one night it would be great.

On his sleeve notes for *Hex,* Smith refers to this track as a 'Desperate attempt to make bouncy good of 2 drum kit line-up' and while the feel of the song veers far closer to 'pounding' than 'bouncy', it definitely depends on a dual drum kit to sustain its attack. In fact it was only ever played live when me and Karl were in the group, apart from a one-off revival in 1997 when it was brought back for a gig at London's Astoria. The Fall performed both the song and concert in tribute to Leo Finlay,[88] the well-

---

[87] This is the Hammersmith Palais performance released on *Hip Priest and Kamerads.* We were supported on the night by The Birthday Party and The Room.

[88] Finlay died tragically young, aged just 32. The gig at Astoria 2 also featured three other favourites of his: Travis, Ash and Formula 1. He was warmly thought of by all who crossed his path – Blur were so grateful for his support early in their career they played at his wedding.

respected music journalist who had died unexpectedly the previous December. 'And This Day' was his favourite Fall song.

The Hitchin recording was brutally edited down – including at the beginning, unusually – to a more manageable 10:23, to make the album come in at almost exactly the hour its title promised. The song starts as if the tape has been switched on after the band have started,[89] and the edit at 5:50 barely manages to synch the beat correctly. Both of these deliberately clumsy edits add to the song's overarching feel of randomness. In a similar way to 'Yer Blues' on The Beatles' *White Album*, the brutality of the editing process is presented as a mark of the song's, and by default the group's, authenticity, but such post-performance tampering is by definition anything but authentic. It's also another example of Mark's messing with a song's timing to throw everyone off the scent. As he revealed in the album's accompanying press release, 'And This Day' was 'savagely and randomly edited to produce new lyrics & impossible notes'.

The lyric is the aural equivalent of *Hex*'s sleeve, its seemingly random non-sequiturs eventually building a complete picture that's probably saying *something,* but is in no mood to reveal exactly what. The whole lyric feels so fragmented it's entirely possible Mark's making it up as he goes along, an example of his previously referenced confession that sometimes 'the words just come off the top of my head'. But if he is ad-libbing, quite what such lines as 'The surroundings are screaming on the roads', 'the body's like a U.S. football player's' and 'no matter what and never who fills baskets' tell us about his preoccupations at the time is anyone's guess. 'Who are the translators?' Braver people than me, that's for sure.

Craig Scanlon: Where 'Winter' and 'Deer Park' are literate 'And This Day' is just Mark ranting, pissed off about getting no respite from whatever – probably spending time with the rest of the band! That's why it went on so long, to convey his horror.

---

[89] The Hammersmith Palais version includes the proper intro – which consists of two bars of solo keyboards before the drums come crashing in.

'And This Day', then, is quite hard work, in many senses.[90] The press release notes that this track 'intends to intimidate the listener into The Fall's intelligence thru noise waves'. Though (or even because) its determined non-musicality and anti-intellectualism veer close to self-parody at times, as a closer for an album as dense as *Hex Enduction Hour*, 'And This Day' is just about perfect. Musically harrowing and lyrically all-but unfathomable, it's the quintessential Fall album track, and as such it makes much less sense in isolation.

Craig Scanlon: Retrospectively, if this was going to be Mark's last LP, then 'no fucking respite' works as a goodbye. It's good and violent, and suited Mark's lyric. It's too fucking long though.

---

[90] Playing it live was no picnic, believe me. It was usually more about endurance than musicality and by the thirteen-minute mark it became something of an out-of-body experience.

[SIDE ONE: TRACK 4a] **Fortress**

Words/Music Burns–Riley–Scanlon-Smith
(Smith/Scanlan/Riley/Burns)

Smith vocal; *Riley* keyboards; *Scanlon* guitar; *Hanley (S)* bass; *Burns*
drums; *Hanley (P)* drums

First played live: 19th May 1981, Markthalle, Hamburg, West Germany

Recorded: December 1981, stage, Regal Cinema, Hitchin

Producer: Richard Mazda. **Engineer:** Tony J. Sutcliffe

Released: 8th March 1982

DREAM OF Gibbous
Synth-men & their BAGS

At a mere one minute and twenty-one seconds,[91] 'Fortress' could be almost be considered as an intro to 'Deer Park' – but it was definitely a song in its own right, and the two were rarely played together live. The decision to record these two songs in one go was inspired – though similar in key and tempo the two songs were different enough to make the transition uniquely thrilling.[92]

Lyrically the two songs are entirely separate, though they do share a common distain for metropolitan media types. But then they're hardly unique amongst Fall lyrics for that.

The song, composed by Craig, consisted of two sections, neither of which could really be called a chorus, and Mark's vocal makes little allowance for the change between sections. The first part is a good example of Craig's ability to successfully blur the line between chords and riffs and as such is a distant cousin to 'Wings'. The second part's vague similarity to songs such as 'Slates' and 'Gut of the Quantifier' is probably what caused Steve to later dismiss the song as 'Fall by numbers'. Even so, the song's brevity means at least it doesn't outstay its welcome.

Apart from the intro, the only other overdub was a pre-recorded cassette Mark had made reciting the lyric while hitting his kitchen table with a stick.

On 14th April 1981, Mark was invited to appear on Adrian Love's *Talkabout*, which was advertised as 'Radio 1's open forum –

---

[91] Nine seconds of which consist of Mark's spoof radio announcement over the Casio VL-1's 'Rock-2' rhythm setting and him chanting 'Oo-way oh – spare (a) little grease'. Launched in 1979, the Casio VL-1 was the first mass produced digital synthesiser, and as such came at a price which made it accessible to the average working musician. Even I could afford one. It boasted several pre-programmed rhythm tracks, a basic sequencer and a calculator. As well as on 'Da Da Da' by Trio, the 'Rock-2' rhythm setting can be heard on 'The Man Whose Head Expanded', where Craig also plays its keyboard. I played it on 'Neighbourhood of Infinity' and 'Eat Y'self Fitter' on *Perverted By Language*. It also appears in the video for 'Eat Y'self Fitter'.
[92] 'Fortress' is (roughly) in A while 'Deer Park' is in A minor.

an opportunity for schools and clubs to choose a subject, provide a panel and pick the programme's music'. On this occasion the club was the Albany Basement Theatre Group of Lewisham.[93] The discussion was recorded at Langham Hotel, an annex of Broadcasting House which was owned by the BBC and in its time not only served as a hotel but also housed a number of recording studios. The conversation was based around the current state of the nation, with the four young amateur actors repeatedly blaming the establishment. Mark was sufficiently vexed by the experience to pen a satisfyingly splenetic lyric which even takes umbrage at the door numbers – CH10CH11 is presumably a parody of the BBC addressing system. All rooms in Langham Hotel were prefixed LH followed by the floor and room number. Broadcasting House rooms begin BH, in Maida Vale it was MV.

In the press release for *Slates*, which was released on 27th April, Mark noted that the recording was made using 'the hip priest approach, aired first on an April Peel session recorded in the Nazi fortress'. Though the dates are a little off (the Peel session was recorded on 24th March and broadcast a week later on the 31st) this was clearly the session alluded to, and it was also recorded in Langham Hotel. Mark uses the backronym 'Boiled Beef and Carrots'[94] to refer to the BBC and occasionally substituted 'BBC' for 'Nazi' in live performance.

Once you're armed with the information about the interview at Langham Hotel, 'Fortress' is revealed as possibly the straightest piece of reportage Mark ever committed to paper. He spends a desperate couple of hours in the company of four naive left-wing youths, and instantly regrets his decision to agree to do the show – he's at a loss as to why he ever signed the contract.[95] He then gets lost amidst the BBC's labyrinthine corridors and ends up having to navigate his way through a crowded toilet, where he

[93] For information about this interview I'm grateful to The Annotated Fall website (see Index of Quotes for details) and particularly the sterling detective work of regular contributor 'dannyno'.

[94] 'Boiled Beef and Carrots' was a popular music hall song composed in 1909, thirteen years before the birth of the BBC. It seems in the intervening sixty years no one else had made the connection between their initials.

[95] If he was required to sign a contract, then by implication he must have been getting paid – though clearly not enough to make his ordeal worthwhile.

bumps into Henry V, or presumably an actor who'd played him, and notorious long-term BBC employee and friend to the royals Sir Jimmy Savile OBE.[96]

Craig Scanlon: The BBC had that ridiculous door-naming thing, which is why we always got lost in Maida Vale.

Despite the song's unusual linear nature, it's always dangerous, and possibly disappointing, to take any of Mark's lyrics at purely face value. It's been argued, for instance, that Langham Hotel, and by implication the BBC, is used here as a metaphor for Great Britain. Mark occasionally alluded to this interpretation on stage: 'I spent time in this institution – it's called Great Britain'[97] but of course he's as guilty of retrospectively adding meaning to his lyrics as anyone.

---

[96] Depending on whether or not there's a semicolon between the two lines, this could be read as 'and good King Harry was there fucking Jimmy Saville'. However, if Mark had witnessed such a notable assignation I'm sure he would have mentioned it elsewhere.
[97] Maxwell's, Hoboken, 4th June 1981.

[SIDE ONE: TRACK 4b] **Deer Park**

Words/Music: Burns-Riley-Scanlon-Smith
(Smith/Scanlan/Riley/Burns)

Smith vocal, guitar; *Riley* keyboards; *Scanlon* guitar; *Hanley (S)* bass; *Burns* drums; *Hanley (P)* drums

First played live: 25th May 1981, Rheinterrassen, Bonn, West Germany

Recorded: December 1981, stage, Regal Cinema, Hitchin

Producer: Richard Mazda. **Engineer:** Tony J. Sutcliffe

Released: 8th March 1982

ACAD. VEGO'S

Marc Riley: I came up with the keyboard part, with the organ on 'A'. That's all that it is.

Craig Scanlon: Mark definitely showed me that guitar line, but we all got a credit,[98] and I think that's fair enough because it's a proper group effort.

'Deer Park' was played several times with either Karl or me behind the kit, but it really came into its own when we started playing together. On 'The Classical' we tackled the dilemma of how to justify two drum kits by playing entirely different patterns. In contrast, on 'Deer Park' we found ourselves locked into a single pattern that propelled the song to heights it never attained when only one or the other of us was playing. You can hear evidence of the difference this made by reviewing both the live performance from *A Part of America Therein*, which only featured Karl, and the version recorded for John Peel two months later that only had me on drums. Though both are perfectly acceptable performances, they pale beside the *Hex* version. What's more, Karl and I not only spurred each other to greater heights, but the rest of the group were similarly galvanised by the thumping groove behind them. The same sense of excitement at what we were creating that pervades 'Fantastic Life' and 'The Classical' is all over 'Deer Park's performance. Which is important, because the success or failure of 'one movement' songs like 'Deer Park' and 'And This Day' is entirely dependent on the execution. There's no falling back on the fact that they're good songs, because deprived of performance they're not really songs at all. All of which makes the decision to record the band on stage a brilliant one. As with

[96] Not quite all.

111

'Iceland', Mark was moved to pick up a guitar and join in, a sure sign that he appreciated what he was hearing.

Asked to contribute to the *NME*'s 'Portrait of the Artist as a Consumer' in August 1981, Mark listed *Ritual in the Dark* by Colin Wilson as one of his 'reads'. As he states in 'Deer Park's chorus, Wilson did indeed write at least some of *Ritual in the Dark* in Chepstow Villas, Notting Hill.[99] The flat was about half a mile from the Rough Trade office. Rough Trade itself was the source of much of Mark's ire in the lyric. The song, at least in part, is as concerned with recounting real events as its predecessor, 'Fortress'.

Discussing *Hex Enduction Hour* on Radio 4's *Saturday Review* with poet Paul Farley in 2008, BBC editor Liz Forgan (who was working at the new Channel 4 when *Hex* was released) revealed she'd hated The Fall ever since the album came out. She described The Fall in 1982 as pouring 'buckets of ordure over every single green shoot of joyfulness or hope, including I think at the time, explicitly Channel 4'. Though neither track actually mentions the new station, it's likely she had this track and 'Fortress' in mind. Farley, who had picked the album to discuss, agreed that at the time the group were 'totally anti-metropolitan'.

Craig Scanlon: 'Deer Park' was an absolutely perfect picture of London at that time.

While we were signed to Rough Trade, whenever we were in London we stayed at the Notting Hill Gate Hotel, which was nearby.[100] It didn't have a bar, so Mark was often to be seen frequenting the nearby off-licences, particularly between the hours of 3pm and 5:30pm. This is where we find him in the first verse of 'Deer Park', having successfully negotiated his way past the punk-rock tourists who regularly frequented Rough Trade's

[99] As it centres round both existential philosophy and a mysterious serial killer who bases himself on Jack the Ripper, it's easy to see why *Ritual in the Dark* appealed to Mark.
[100] It was damp, absolutely filthy and served inedible breakfasts. But it did boast rooms that slept four, which was inevitably where Steve, Craig, Marc and I ended up. Whenever I hear the 'one room' line in 'Leave The Capitol' I am immediately transported back there, unfortunately.

record shop. One can only imagine his irritation at having to wait while the student in front of him counts out his shrapnel to see if he has enough for two whole cans of lager.

Having finally been served, Mark turns his withering attention to Rough Trade itself. As we've seen, his disdain for Rough Trade's staff was so acute it was always going to end up in a lyric. He had particular contempt for what he perceived as their lazy working practices – much like his band, Mark saw them as employees, and so expected them to put in the day's work that was so evidently beyond him.

Steve Hanley: The story that Geoff Travis told about Mark standing outside the label offices in the morning making sure everyone was clocking in on time[101] is absolute bollocks. As if he'd ever get it together to be standing on the street at 9am.

The line 'fat Captain Beefheart imitators with zits' is thought by some to refer to the group Pere Ubu, who were also on Rough Trade and whose guitarist had helped produce *Grotesque*.[102]

Mark's irritation with the 'sleeping promo dept' would return to haunt him when we re-signed to Rough Trade in 1983 – they had apparently woken up and were teeming with ideas. Unfortunately, their efforts were focused squarely in raising the profile of The Smiths. Unlike the unnamed Manchester band referred to in 'Deer Park', The Smiths' experience was, at least initially, exactly what they thought it should be. This was doubly humiliating for Mark – he was less than thrilled at having to slink back to Rough Trade at all, let alone to play second fiddle to The Smiths. To make matters worse, The Smiths also had first refusal on Grant Showbiz's time as a live sound mixer.

The title of the song is taken from another book Mark listed in the *NME* 'Portrait of the Artist as a Consumer' feature, *The Deer Park* by Norman Mailer. The original 'Deer Park' was the name

---

[101] As reported in the *Guardian*, 29th November 2018.
[102] To those who, with some justification, point out that this description could apply equally to The Fall, I can only say this: thanks in part to the Notting Hill Gate's chef, we very definitely weren't fat.

Louis XV gave to his personal bordello, and Mailer used it to illustrate the depraved goings-on at a fictionalised Palm Springs. Mark transposes the metaphor to best describe the middle-class hipsters slumming it in the previously staunchly working-class district of West 11. Similarly to his disdain for someone who would buy just two cans of lager, he is particularly contemptuous of those who got 'a sex thrill out of a sixteenth of Moroccan'. He had no time for anyone who couldn't handle what they were ingesting.

Richard Mazda: Mark always had an edge – he could have had some magic mushrooms and several lines of speed washed down with several pints of bitter, but he'd still be there telling people to 'keep it together – stop talking too much'.

Who is the King Shag Corpse?

This line has prompted endless speculation; it is often thought to refer to Ian Curtis, the late Joy Division singer, and other theories have it pointing to Elvis Presley, known as the King 'Shag' is a British slang word that means 'fuck', one which has gained a certain amount of traction in the United States in the wake of the *Austin Powers* franchise. There is also a bird native to New Zealand called a Rough-Faced Shag which is also often referred to as a King Shag, which probably has little to do with the song, but may have planted the phrase in MES's mind. – *The Annotated Fall*

'Who is the king shag corpse?' wondered Mark E. Smith in 1981. Most likely he had the cult of Ian Curtis on his mind. – **Bob Stanley**

Of course, deciphering the message has always been part of The Fall's appeal and although in slower, more contemplative numbers like 'Tempo House' we might eventually work out why the Dutch are weeping, the jury remains undecided on the vital question of 'Who IS the King Shag Corpse?' – *Perfect Sound Forever*

It's fascinating that Ian Curtis has become the prime suspect in this particular game of Cluedo, despite there being no evidence in either the rest of 'Deer Park's lyric or from anything Mark said at the time, that the 'King Shag Corpse' was the recently deceased Joy Division singer. It's true that the line doesn't really have anything to do with the rest of the song, so it's not impossible Mark was referring to someone unrelated to Rough Trade, West 11 or London. But Curtis wasn't possessed of notably high sexual appetites, as far as we know. So the only reason to suspect Mark was referring to him is that he could have been expected to say *something* about the passing of another prominent Manchester

(1 hr)   (1 hr)   (1 hr)

MESSAGE FOR YER...

HAIL THE CLASSICAL

ARE YOU STILL...
- ☐ bowing to 'Mythical Thingy'?
- ☐ in need of that 'one true sentence'?
- ☐ wondering who is the 'King Shag Corpse'?

Then you <u>still</u> need the HEXAN school.
Lay down your weary trend <u>now</u>.   HERE'S HOW...

CIGS SMOKED HERE

UNSUITABLE FOR ROMANTICS

HEX ENDUCTION HOUR
HEXEN BY THE FALL

WHO MAKES THE NAZIS?

JAWBONE AND THE AIR-RIFLE

AND MANY MORE!

CUT OUT

* Fabulous stereo effects
* 2 drum kit line-up
* immortal melodies
* chummy lifestyle tips
* euro-processed vinyl

AND FILE AWAY FOR REFERENCE

THINK FIRST - MOST DOKTORS FOLLOW WHAT'S 'BEST'

KAMERA
RECORDS

DISTRIBUTED BY STAGE 1 RECORDS   KAM 005

writer/singer, and that Curtis was a now a corpse. In fact, Mark had already addressed Ian's demise – and explicitly – on the version of 'Cash 'n' Carry' from *A Part of America Therein*:

> Even in Manchester – there's two types of factory there. One makes men old corpses – they stumble round like lost dogs. One lives off old dying men, one lives off the back of a dead man. You know which one, you know which Factory I mean.

No coy unanswered questions there, and it's clear Mark's contempt was reserved for the record label. It's unlikely he'd have referred to someone who'd recently died in such tragic circumstances so crassly.

In fact, the answer to the question 'Who is the King Shag Corpse?' is probably much more prosaic and throwaway, and to be found much closer to home. As far as I was concerned at the time, 'King Shag' was Karl Burns (for obvious reasons) and 'The King Shag Corpse' was a subsequent title Mark bestowed on Grant Showbiz. And as Grant replied when I put that particular theory to him: 'That fits with my memory. Let's face it, we were the only ones… I think they said "getting some" back in the day, as alluded to in Steve's lovely book.'

He did have one important caveat to my assigning of roles however… 'It was the other way round.' So there you go. Karl or Grant. But definitely not Ian Curtis.

[SIDE ONE: TRACK 5] **Mere Pseud Mag. Ed.**

Words: Smith **Music:** Riley

(Smith)

Smith vocal; *Riley* guitar; *Scanlon* guitar; *Hanley (S)* bass, vocals; *Burns* drums; *Hanley (P)* drums

First played live: 12th March 1982, Bristol Polytechnic

Recorded: December 1981, stage, Regal Cinema, Hitchin

Producer: Richard Mazda. **Engineer:** Tony J. Sutcliffe

Released: 8th March 1982

POOR-PROCESS

'Mere Pseud' is one of only two songs worked up at Bury New Road that had never been played live before it was taped for *Hex*. It was originally rehearsed with Karl on his own, and at the next rehearsal Karl turned up late to find us playing the song with the 'on' and 'off' beats reversed. None of the band had noticed.[103]

Marc Riley: I love that song – it was Mark's tune. The riff was ripped off from 'Baby Sitters' by Stupid Babies,[104] which was Adamski when he was eleven years old.[105] It was a great record, about a minute and a half long. It was on one of the Fast records *Earcom* compilations and I think we nicked a copy from Alan Horne at Postcard Records.[106] They used the same distribution as Fast and had a little depot there. Mark showed me the riff on two fingers on his little plastic guitar. That was at his flat in Prestwich, which I went back to recently. That was a strange feeling, a lot of weird and wonderful things went on there.

Like several songs on *Hex Enduction Hour*, it's striking that no one felt the need to expand on the original riff. It's increasingly rare to find such unselfconscious non-musicality on record, and its prevalence in post-punk is perhaps the genre's greatest gift. 'Mere Pseud' is also a good example of Mark's stated intention

---

[103] I still say it sounded better my way round, but Karl's interpretation prevailed, of course.

[104] It's interesting to note the credits with that in mind. Mark could legitimately claim to have written the whole of the music himself, and on the label of the record the song is credited to him alone. However, according to the PRS database the music was composed entirely by Marc Riley. While it's possible Mark made a mistake when filing the paperwork, I don't think we can disregard the notion that he put Marc in the frame in case Stupid Babies' publishers started asking awkward questions.

[105] Born Adam Tinley, Adamski's biggest hit was 1990's 'Killer' which featured Seal on vocals.

[106] Bob Last's Fast records released three *Earcom* compilations in 1979. By far the most famous is *Earcom 2* as it featured two tracks by Joy Division that were unavailable elsewhere. 'Baby Sitters' was on *Earcom 3*.

to mess with the timings of songs – his vocals follow the same melody line as the guitars but never at the same time. The song itself has absolutely no intention of keeping a steady pace either, so remaining in synch for the duration of the middle eight's ever-increasing tempo was quite a challenge for Karl and me. But the resulting sonic bombardment was well worth the effort.

Craig Scanlon: Live it was absolutely brilliant – the full powerhouse, all one noise. When you got it right the two drummers were stunning live. But on *Hex* it was too similar to come straight after 'Fortress/Deer Park'. They should have been broken up.

It's never entirely clear whether the subject of the song is someone pretentious who edits a magazine[107] or his father, or even the father commenting on the son. While the real ale, Spanish guitar and beard would point to the pseud magazine editor, the bulk of the protagonist's preoccupations – Weetabix, darts, *Not the Nine O'Clock News*, *Rumpole of the Bailey* and double-entendre, are more down-to-earth preoccupations. It's entirely possible that this was just what was on the telly the day Mark wrote it. But Mark's thinly-veiled contempt for journalists, with their 'fancied wit' and unforgivable inability to put their hands in their pockets, is ever-present. Pointing out that the protagonist 'had a weak pisser' seems a little unkind, but it's always rewarding to hear Mark berate some unfortunate who's earned his scorn, even if we're not sure why, or even if he deserves it.

'Mere Pseud Mag. Ed.' was evidently a favourite of Mark's – a live version from 1983 was included on 1985's *Hip Priest and Kamerads* compilation, and the song continued to make sporadic appearances in the group's setlist throughout the eighties and nineties. Between 2002 and 2004 it was a regular part of the set – in fact during that period the group played it live over 60 times, far more than the *Hex* line-up ever managed. They also recorded surprisingly faithful versions for the *John Peel Show* in

[105] Or someone who edits a pretentious magazine, of course.

February 2003 and for the *Interim* album in 2004. The fact that the song was played by so many different Fall line-ups would indicate that Mark felt it belonged solely to him – whatever the registered credits say. It's an unlikely set perennial which makes no attempt at being a crowd pleaser – even if it ended up being one purely by dint of its number of appearances. Long-term fans, buoyed by a rare bit of nostalgia, who attempted a sing-a-long were likely to remain frustrated – the wayward timing would defeat you even if you could get your mouth round the 'Mere pseud mag editor's father' refrain. The song made its final live appearance on the 12th March 2005 – exactly 23 years to the day from its debut performance. Like 'Hip Priest' it was played by all line-ups except the final two.

SKRIKKING KIDS

Once 'The Classical', 'And This Day', 'Fortress/Deer Park' and 'Mere Pseud' had been committed to tape, a collective decision was made to move everyone to the recording studio upstairs, which was where Mark had been doing his vocals all along. As the rest of the songs needed either a more intimate setting or a degree of studio sophistication, this was a wise move. It also meant that the five of us who were previously stuck out there in the cinema could stop moaning about the cold.

There's a discernible change in sound and atmosphere between the two sessions, though it's largely disguised by *Hex*'s final running order, and it was obviously never picked up on by those eager to perpetuate the myth that the whole thing was taped in an abandoned theatre. There's also a persuasive school of thought, which Craig for one subscribes to, that the songs recorded in the studio sound better. However, it's doubtful that the actual *performances* of the songs recorded on the stage could ever have been achieved in a normal studio situation. The loss in fidelity of sound is more than made up for by the sheer intensity of the musicians' performance, literally live on stage. In the end, the dividing of the recordings between stage and studio matched the respective songs so perfectly that it's one of the key elements of the album's success.

[SIDE ONE: TRACK 2] **Jawbone and the Air-Rifle**

Words: Smith **Music:** Hanley (S)-Riley-Scanlon-Smith
(Smith/The Fall)

Smith vocal; *Riley* guitar, vocal; *Scanlon* guitar, vocal; *Hanley (S)* bass;
Burns drums; *Hanley (P)* drums

First played live: 29th August 1980, Railway Working Men's Club,
Nelson

Recorded: December 1981, studio, Regal Cinema, Hitchin

Producer: Richard Mazda. **Engineer:** Tony J. Sutcliffe

Released: 8th March 1982

Slogger GelatiNe-Gut HAcks

The oldest song on the album, 'Jawbone and the Air-Rifle' was composed in the summer of 1980, and completed at a writing session at Mark and Kay's flat with Mark, Marc, Craig and Steve in attendance.

Marc Riley: Mark said to Craig that he wanted something like 'Run Rabbit Run' to fit his lyrics.[108] We wrote it in my bedroom.

In response to Craig's verse, Marc came up with a chorus riff that, unusually for The Fall, obeyed the rules of pop and neatly matched Mark's lyric syllable for syllable. The song was worked-up with drums a few days later at T J Davidson's on Little Peter Street, during a rehearsal that had been convened ahead of a return to live performance after nearly a month off. The lengthy delay between its genesis and eventual recording wasn't an indicator that 'Jawbone' needed work: live recordings of its earliest outings show that both lyric and structure were mostly locked in from the start. The main change between its earlier incarnation and the version on *Hex* is the addition of Craig's wonderfully expressive guitar part on the two breaks.

Craig Scanlon: It's a good riff but it's dead clunky, there's certain riffs that just sound natural, but I suppose if you're told to play 'Run Rabbit Run' it's going to be a bit clunky.

'Jawbone' was recorded a number of times before the definitive version was committed to tape in the studio of the Regal Cinema. As well as the version recorded for John Peel's show in 1980, and

---

[108] Popularised by Flanagan & Allen, 'Run Rabbit Run' was supposedly a favourite of Winston Churchill's during World War II.

the version released on *Live in London*, an attempt was made at Cabaret Voltaire's Western Works studio on 27th February 1981, the day before both groups were scheduled to play a benefit for the Leadmill in Sheffield. No one was particularly impressed with the results and nothing from this session has ever seen the light of day.

'Jawbone and the Air-Rifle' is one of Mark's most successful 'story' songs, and a really good example of what he called 'the mundane everyday as a backdrop for great terror'. The narrative is linear and coherent and tells a fully fleshed-out tale which details both a troubled marriage and arcane malignance. He clearly took a lot of effort with the lyric – unlike earlier excursions into this genre such as 'New Face in Hell' and 'The N.W.R.A.'. 'Jawbone and the Air-Rifle' manages to couch its narrative in a song that mostly sticks to the rules of pop-song structure. One notable exception to this is the fourth verse's extra bar, inserted to allow the origins of the curse ('Formed on a Scotch Island to make you a bit of a man') to be clearly enunciated without the gabbling necessary on the Peel version.[109]

The story plays out like an episode of Mark's favourite *The Twilight Zone*: an unemployed man turned poacher uses a nocturnal rabbit hunt as an excuse to get away from his family, with unfortunate consequences. The Annotated Fall website speculates, with some credibility, that the song is set where Prestwich Clough backs onto the North Manchester Synagogue and its adjacent cemetery.

The poacher misshoots and chips a headstone. At this point the gravekeeper appears, and there are definite echoes of *Hamlet*'s gravedigger in his exchange with the would-be rabbit killer.[110] We're given no clue as to why the gravekeeper's working at night, so it's possible that the poacher's second instinct is correct and

[109] Alas there still isn't room to replace the word 'Scotch' with the correct two-syllabled adjective 'Scottish'.
[110] Mark had scant regard for the quality of the English tuition he received – he was particularly disgusted by his English teachers' lack of literary knowledge ('What about Norman Mailer? Or Henry Miller? The teacher had never heard of them.') but *Hamlet* was one of the works he did study. Note also the iambic pentameter of lines such as 'And said goodbye to his infertile spouse', 'And the gravekeeper was out on his rounds' and 'Carried air rifle and firm stock of wood'.

the person before him is posing as a gravekeeper to further his criminal intent.[111] If this was true it would make the singer an unreliable narrator – a literary convention that's rarely used by other lyricists, though Mark used it highly effectively.

The gravekeeper commands the poacher to move where he can see him, which is quite brave, given that he's talking to a man with a gun who's evidently not afraid to use it. As it happens, it's the poacher who is terrified of the gravekeeper, and, suitably cowed, he divulges his miserable life story with little or no encouragement.

Clearly suffering from depression, the rabbit-killer reveals that he's an unemployed husband and father of four. This revelation has prompted no small degree of discussion amongst aficionados of Mark's lyrics, as we're told at the beginning of the song that his wife is infertile. This could, of course, be a new development, but there's more than a hint that in this case 'infertile' is code for 'uninterested in sex'. The rabbit-killer cannot find gratification in his family and nor is he able to 'drink to forget' – drinking makes him feel worse, so instead he leaves his house at night to shoot wildlife. 'There's been no war for forty years' is a curious piece of self-justification – perhaps he thinks his nocturnal hobby would seem less strange if rationing were in place and he could sell his game on the black market. It's also possible that the rabbit-killer feels inadequate when compared to the greatest generation. It's only conjecture, but this may be a glimpse into Mark's own views of his and his generation's inadequacy, especially in contrast to his forbears' fortitude in the face of annihilation.

Mark E. Smith: It's pathetic. I'd like to see them at war. It's a generational thing – something's amiss with too many lads these days around the ages of thirty-five and under.

Is Mark's dismissal of the younger generation's unsuitability for

[111] The gravekeeper had every right to be disgruntled, as the poacher was wildly reckless when it came to discharging his weapon. 'I thought you were rabbit prey, or a loose sex-criminal' is a pretty poor excuse – whatever he thought he saw it could hardly have been an either-or between a rabbit and a pervert.

armed conflict a veiled piece of self-analysis? It's possible, because despite his frequent references to his dad's stint in the army and his assertion that one of his relatives served at Rorke's Drift,[112] Mark obviously had no more experience of military life than the people he was criticising.

The gravekeeper rewards the poacher for his candour with a gift in the shape of a cursed jawbone, and the rabbit-killer soon discovers that war-war would probably have been preferable to jaw-jaw. In his 2018 article for *The Quietus,* 'The Fall and Mark E. Smith as a Narrative Lyric Writer', Taylor Parkes has postulated that the gravekeeper gives him a sheep's jawbone, salvaged from 'Gruinard, site of bio-weapon tests in the Second World War, and its "curse" may be of a more prosaic nature'. He bases this theory on the subtitle the song is given in the published lyric book: 'A wee tale from the Anthrax Isle', but there's nothing in the lyric itself to suggest that the jawbone is anything but human ('a bit of a man'), though not necessarily from the graveyard where they're standing. In San Francisco on 12th July 1981, Mark introduced the song thus: 'All Scottish Presbyterians on uncharted islands rule by iron fist and the curses that can evoke from trigger happy boys.'[113]

According to TheFall.org gigography, on the 27th October 1981, Mark presaged the song with 'Right, this is a little story about Miss Andreck's tomb. Tragic life.' There's no indication of who Miss Andreck is, and it's possible it could be a mondegreen, Andreck/anthrax aren't too far apart. But who knows? In any case, the cursed jawbone begins affecting the poacher almost straightaway. He immediately loses his appetite, followed by his courage, his teeth and eventually his mind. Like those Warner Brothers cartoons where the starving protagonist sees food wherever he looks, the rifleman's hallucinations take the form of anthropomorphised jawbones. Whether through exposure to arcane forces or anthrax, it's implied the poacher meets a sticky end.

---

[112] Alfred Henry Hook VC, played somewhat unsympathetically in the film *Zulu* by James Booth.

[113] Beats 'this is our new single, hope you like it' doesn't it?

Mark's willingness to bend his language to rhyme and the metre of the song is surprisingly rewarding – there's a poetic feel to the dialogue that contrasts nicely with his more prose-heavy writing. Mark shows he's a dab hand with the poetic conventions of internal rhyme ('night sight') and alliteration, of which 'wreath-roots' is a striking example, not least because wreaths don't normally have roots. His economy of language throughout is also worth noting – when describing the tombstone, he uses the single word 'valued' to suggest both expense and sentimental attachment. Also, the poacher's story is neatly summed up in the last word of each chorus – while the jawbone remains 'cursed' every time, the air-rifle goes from 'borne' to 'warm' (i.e. fired)[114] to 'gone'.

Unlike many songs on the album, the various sections are of a set length, the notable exceptions being when Mark abandons metre for the two spoken middle-eight sections. His wilfully indeterminate phrasing on these breaks meant that the transition back into the verse and chorus respectively was always a matter of interpretation. You can hear the difficulty this presented on the version recorded for John Peel in 1980, where the roll into the last chorus comes mid-bar and causes some not inconsiderable timing issues.[115]

Steve Hanley: It was impossible to get right!

Marc Riley: There was always terror in everyone's eyes, coming out of the break. You can hear the panic!

Craig Scanlon: Two years playing it and we still couldn't get it right.

---

[114] As John Lennon pointed out when asked to explain the title of his song – 'a warm gun means you've just shot something'.

[115] There was no way to quantify how long the breaks would last, it was different every time. As a drummer you just had to know the words and second-guess Mark, who insisted the change came as soon as he finished saying 'laid off work' and 'energy from the mainland' respectively. It was no good trying to explain that the drum roll had to be a certain length and come at the right musical jump-off point. He didn't give a fuck about any of that nonsense.

In keeping with the arc of the album, the two breaks are taken at a noticeably slower tempo. As both these sections take us into the poacher's internal monologue, the change of pace emphasises his distracted state as he slowly loses his mind and succumbs to visions of 'Wicker Man'-type ceremonies, jarringly transported to the rifleman's distinctly urban location ('the villagers dance round pre-fabs').[116]

Karl was originally charged with drumming on the album version, but possibly because he was less willing to bend to Mark's idiosyncratic notions of timing, immediately before recording Mark decided that I should play it, with Karl coming in on the two breaks and after the final chorus. This meant my original plan, to play bongos in the style of 'Do or Die' from The Human League's recently-released album *Dare* was scuppered.[117] That I didn't attempt to add them later would suggest my idea was more about giving myself something to do than enhancing the track. In fact, the finished recording featured very little in the way of embellishment. Marc and Craig overdubbed the voice of the gravekeeper ('You're out of luck') and the 'jawbone and the air-rifle' chant on the breaks, but Mark's vocal was recorded live. 'Jawbone' was, by dint of its familiarity, relatively straightforward, and the recording was completed very quickly.

Craig Scanlon: The chorus is a bit football-crowd as well.

Marc Riley: 'Jawbone' was quite straight, but it's a great pop song, in the most off-kilter way – it's not 'Agadoo' is it? And amid all *Hex*'s bombs going off it's almost a bit of light relief.

---

[116] There was an entire estate of pre-fab houses in Heaton Park, Prestwich, when Mark was growing up. Originally built as temporary housing at the end of the Second World War, they were still there in the seventies.

[117] Like much of the country I was obsessed with *Dare* from the minute it was released, particularly the drums, which I initially couldn't believe were created by a drum machine. I bought a Casio VL-1 mini keyboard as a direct result of Phil Oakey's revelation that they'd used one throughout the album.

[SIDE TWO: TRACK 3] **Who Makes The Nazis?**

Words/Music: Smith

(Smith)

Smith vocal; *Riley* guitar; *Scanlon* guitar; *Hanley (S)* bass, vocals; *Hanley (P)* drums; *Burns* tapes

First played live: 4th September 1981, Sheffield Polytechnic

Recorded: December 1981, studio, Regal Cinema, Hitchin

Producer: Richard Mazda. **Engineer:** Tony J. Sutcliffe

Released: 8th March 1982

CUSHY E.E.C EURO-STATE GOALS

'Who Makes The Nazis?' was composed by Mark on the open strings of his plastic four-string guitar, which was tuned to something approaching standard bass guitar tuning. The riff was showed to Steve, Marc and Craig at a writing session at his flat in Prestwich. The first time it was played as a full song by us all was at the recording of a Peel session on 26th August 1981.

The choice of tracks recorded for this particular session is a particularly good example of just how different The Fall were from most other bands. They[118] had several new songs that had been thoroughly road tested and honed over the course of a massive American tour, but Mark only chose to perform one of these – for the rest he was happy to take a decidedly more exoteric direction.

Marc Riley: Mark would always view Peel sessions as 'work in progress'. I mean look at 'Hassle Schmuck' – that wasn't even work in progress, it was no work whatsoever.

Steve Hanley: There was never a sense of 'Are people going to like this?' He didn't give a fuck. Those were the days – no rehearsal, just go in and do it. Great.

The absolute lack of bottom end in the music as presented was what prompted the tom-heavy drum pattern. It was a pretty obvious addition, as the timbre of the song was gossamer light, consisting as it did of nothing more than two fairly thin-sounding guitars and a plastic ukulele. Without something substantial to tether it down the music was in danger of floating away. You'll also notice the song contains not a single drum roll – perhaps I was trying to show I was still the kind of drummer Mark preferred.

[118] And it was very much *they* at this point, which wasn't the most pleasant of feelings.

As well as making him play a toy, Mark also caused Steve further embarrassment by picking him to perform the vocal interjection from 'Bobby'. In a remarkably prescient impression of a far-right politician, Bobby extols the virtues of soft-soaping your prospective voters rather than hurling rocks, while making it clear that division and hatred remain his central tenet.

More than sufficiently mortified by his vocal interjection, Steve was determined that he wouldn't be stuck playing a plastic ukulele live on stage. He worked out a rough approximation of Mark's riff using the harmonics on his bass, and by the time it came to be recorded the song had been played live at least a dozen times and was sounding much more robust. Both the tribal drums and Marc and Craig's guitar counter-melodies worked much better with the harmonics, as luck would have it.

One key element of *Hex*'s version of 'Who Makes The Nazis?' was the cassette tape that appears every so often. This was operated by Karl, in real time, and played through a vocal mic. Mark used this technique on several Fall recordings, and often these were tapes of Mark's earliest renderings of his idea for the song itself, which is probably the case here. Obviously, no attempt was made to synch the sounds on the tape to the actual song, and as usual with Mark's taped interjections, you can't really hear what's going on. As noted by Robert Walker in *Mark E. Smith and The Fall: Art, Music and Politics*:

> The taped effects growl away ignorant of the song's rhythm and balance of instruments ... They are not distinct as sounds themselves but become a defined instrument in their own right, the tape recorder. The Dictaphone's tonal characteristics dominate the sounds it has captured to the extent that it becomes more of an instrument than whatever generated them in the first place.

With a title as strong as 'Who Makes The Nazis?' there's a temptation to view every line of the lyric as somehow directly related to answering the question. But assuming such a preciseness of meaning is often a mistake with Mark's lyrics, and it's particularly dangerous here. 'Benny's cobweb eyes' is a jokey reference to the be-hatted brummie from ATV's *Crossroads*, and 'Remember when I used to follow you home from school babe? Before I got picked up for paedophilia' is, according to The Annotated Fall at least, a dig at Big Star's song 'Thirteen'.[119] It's difficult to connect either of those to the rise of the far right (though soap operas and paedophilia, like fascism itself, refuse to die), but possibly not as difficult as working out what 'buffalo lips on toast, smiling' could tell us about the architects of fascism.

Of course the lyric does make some attempts to answer its own question, which, by the way, is not an attempt to rationalise history. It's 'Who *Makes* The Nazis?', not who *made* them. Mark cites TV bias, and does so by making up his own abbreviation – 'telly V', just because he can. He also blames 'all the 'O's'; with 'winos' and 'spermos' as examples. While it's tempting to pinpoint the nature of spermos' addiction by extrapolating from winos' reliance on the fruit of the vine, it's far from guaranteed.

The Irish get a mention, perhaps related to the 'mick slyness' that Mark specifically attached to John F. Kennedy on 'The Man Whose Head Expanded'. In that context, the 'Joe' mentioned here could be Joseph Kennedy, JFK's father.

Mark's opinion of the Nazis themselves, which he saves for the chorus, is at first glance rather clearer: cattle, essentially. But it's doubtful he merely wanted a metaphor for unquestioning obedience, because Longhorns don't quite fit the bill. Texas Longhorns, for example, are known not only for their diverse colouring but also their intelligence. They're also commonly held up as an exemplary illustration of the wonders of natural selection. Maybe that's the point, and the reasons people become Nazis, like Mark's lyrics, are far more complicated than they first appear.

[119] Formed by Alex Chilton, formerly of The Box Tops, Big Star were a massively influential early American powerpop band who never made it quite as big as they possibly deserved. Chilton went on to play with Tav Falco's Panther Burns.

[SIDE TWO: TRACK 2] **Just Step S'ways**

Words/Music: Smith

(Smith)[120]

Smith vocal; *Riley* guitar, vocal; *Scanlon* guitar; *Hanley (S)* bass; *Burns* drums; *Hanley (P)* drums; *Carroll* backing vocals

First played live: 21st October 1981, Xtreems, New Regent, Brighton

Recorded: December 1981, studio, Regal Cinema, Hitchin

Producer: Richard Mazda. **Engineer:** Tony J. Sutcliffe

Released: 8th March 1982

---

[120] It's surprising this passed without comment at the time, especially from Marc, as Mark didn't write a note of 'Just Step S'ways'. Like every other element, his melody line follows Marc's riff.

Lung-Wurm back-Rays

'Just Step S'ways' was one of the first songs written specifically for two drummers, it was worked up during the now six-piece line-up's first UK tour and made its debut in Brighton in October 1981. The main part of the song was written by Marc, Steve added the break.

Marc Riley: That's one of the best things I've ever written. The best thing about it is the staggered repeated phrase following it on a beat later. I must have nicked it off another record, but I don't know where. And the vocals are phrased around the riff.

Craig Scanlon: It was a simple tune, but it had that really good repeat, almost like Motown or 'Row Row Row Your Boat'.[121]

The sheer catchiness of Marc's riff is clear from the fact that everyone who appears on the song, apart from the drummers, plays the same refrain in one form or another. This includes both Marc and Kay's backing vocals and the lead vocal. Because of this, it's likely that the lyric didn't exist in any form before Mark had heard the music. And there aren't many songs where Mark so completely tailored the metre of his lyric to fit the tune. Furthermore, no one dared to add a countermelody for fear it would detract from the main phrase. Because everyone's locked into that same riff, the release that comes with the break, when everyone starts doing something different, is tangible.

The introduction consists of two Mark E. Smiths going head-to-head until the meaning of both phrases is deliberately obscured, though one of the vocals makes explicit reference to the Hip Priest. The intro also features a brief double-tracked vocal brass section by Mark.

[121] The drum pattern is obviously indebted to Motown too.

Craig Scanlon: Mark had this brilliant production technique where there's three or four voices going. When it came to his vocals, he was a good producer.

Robert Walker outlines the importance of this technique in *Mark E. Smith and The Fall: Art, Music and Politics*:

> When The Fall put two or more disparate ... voices into one song, the effect is often alienating because of this fragmentation of time, space and personality.

Mark's previously mentioned predilection for adding what's on the telly into his composition is present and correct – his disdain for celebrities eking out past glories is compared to being in a Hovis advert. There's some debate as to whether Mark's reference to 'Futurists', both here and in the lyric to 'Deer Park', refers to *Futurisimo*, the Italian equivalent of Vorticism (which got further into bed with fascism than either Lewis or Pound dared) or New Romantics – 'Futurists' was one of the early delineations the press gave them. No doubt Mark would have enjoyed the ambiguity. He also references Elton John's 1979 tour of the Soviet Union, with no obvious criticism apparent, and 'lung-worm back-rays', a possible metaphor for lung cancer. Mark was obviously pleased with the line – it's the only one of *Hex*'s lyrics to appear on the front sleeve.

As well as mentioning the album's main character, 'Just Step S'ways' is also the only song which makes any reference to the idea that *Hex* is The Fall's last work – 'His commercial last chance.'

Once again, if you've figured out the lyrical arc of this particular number, you know more than me. Not that it matters anyway – far better to just delight in the myriad twists and turns in Mark's thought processes that are necessitated by having a set melody and thus a limited number of syllables to play with. As with 'Jawbone and the Air-Rifle', Mark's embracing of the strictures of pop took him in an interesting direction. Given its efficacy it's perhaps surprising he didn't do it more often.

[Single/B] I'm Into C.B.

Words/Music: Smith

(Smith)

Smith vocal; *Riley* keyboards; *Scanlon* guitar; *Hanley (S)* bass; *Burns* drums; *Hanley (P)* drums

First played live: 7th December 1981, The Venue, London (though Mark had used the lyrics over various other tunes previously).

Recorded: December 1981, studio, Regal Cinema, Hitchin

Producer: Richard Mazda. **Engineer:** Tony J. Sutcliffe

Released: 19th April 1982

[Single/A] Look, Know

Words: Smith **Music:** Burns-Carroll-Hanley (S)-Riley-Smith[122]

(Smith/Hanley (S)/Burns/Riley)

Smith vocal; *Riley* guitar, vocals; *Scanlon* guitar; *Hanley (S)* bass; *Burns* drums; *Hanley (P)* drums; *Carroll* keyboards

First played live: 4th September 1981, Sheffield Polytechnic, Sheffield

Recorded: December 1981, studio, Regal Cinema, Hitchin

Producer: Richard Mazda. **Engineer:** Tony J. Sutcliffe

Released: 19th April 1982

---

[122] It's curious that Kay was given a credit with the PRS and not on the label, especially considering that as a non-PRS member she never got any money from it anyway.

CHUMMY LIFESTYLE

'I'm Into C.B.' is one of those tracks that neatly sum up The Fall – it features many of the traits that Fall detractors find most annoying, and Fall fans find most appealing. This was nicely illustrated by Stewart Lee's recollection of when he first heard it.

> 'I'm Into C.B.' seemed impossibly annoying. There was no chorus. There was no middle eight. Two guitar chords slashed around its vast formless space. A xylophone beat out a single note throughout. A man shouted incomprehensible stream-of-consciousness lyrics, making no concession to conventional notions of singing. It went on for six and a half minutes, and the band's occasional extemporisations around the restrictive structure seemed to betray apparent frustration rather than joy. I thought it was one of the worst things I had ever heard.

Is there any wonder The Fall soon became an overriding obsession? He was quite correct about the song's musical structure – it's almost impossibly cloying and features incredibly little in the way of progression, apart from Karl's drums. I played the one-handed snare pattern that starts the song and continues unchanged for the next six minutes plus. Mark came up with that, along with the one note everyone, including him, hits pretty much throughout. It's quite striking how little anyone deviates – and also how much authentic tension can be built up when everyone's playing that one note like they really mean it.

Unusually, Mark makes a half-decent stab at a rhyming structure, but on its own that's hardly enough to elevate 'I'm Into C.B.' into an actual song. What really makes the track impressive is the massive sound – Richard captured the group at its very best, and it's telling that this is one of the songs recorded after we moved upstairs to the studio.

The UK craze for Citizens Band radio was at its most intense in 1981, though it was ironically, if not entirely unpredictably, dealt a death-blow when it was legalised on 2nd November. Quite what moved legions of house-based UK twenty-somethings to 'get their ears on' and go 'wall to wall and treetop tall' in the style of US truckers is anyone's guess, but it was certainly popular. One unfortunate side effect of the illegal CB wavelengths was that it could often be picked up on home radiograms, particularly if the CBer was in close proximity. Steve and Marc had many a post-pub listening session ruined by our neighbour Gary 'Superchef' Hood assaulting the airwaves with 'Breaker breaker 1-9' in a broad Manchester accent as they tried to listen to *Street Hassle* or *1969*. Our subsequent tales of his ridiculous and often hilarious combination of witless Wythenshavian and wildly misplaced truck-driver patois directly fed into Mark's lyric for 'I'm Into C.B.'. Given that, the text is really quite sympathetic, and no one is treated too harshly. But the protagonist does make explicit reference to 'New Face in Hell', so maybe he's a Fall fan.

★★★

Though 'Look, Know' was the only song committed to tape at both of the sessions that made up *Hex Enduction Hour*'s recording, it wasn't included on the final album. Instead it was released as a stand-alone single a month after *Hex*. Like 'Who Makes The Nazis?' it was also recorded (as 'Know Look') before it was ever played live, for the John Peel session at Maida Vale on 26th August. The group had worked it up in soundchecks on the American tour and we briefly rehearsed it the day before the session. Try as I might, I couldn't work out how Karl had dealt with the extra beat coming out of the break, so I had to stop playing and then join back in. When I got the chance to ask him I was expecting a fully-deserved dressing down for my inability to cope with an irregular time signature. 'I stopped playing and joined back in,' he admitted.

'Look, Know' went into the live set immediately after the Peel session, so by the third time it was recorded, in Hitchin, it was fully formed and well bedded in.[123] It was mostly written by Steve, though Marc added some guitar at the end he later admitted was inspired by The Fire Engine's 'Candyskin'. It also features some faintly ridiculous interjections on the Casio VL-1 from Kay who was clearly having issues dealing with its mini-keyboard. The drums, which originated with Karl, are for the most part played by me, with Karl only joining in for the outro. This reverses 'Lie Dream's set up, which had Karl playing my original part. It would definitely have been Mark's decision to do it that way, but whether getting us to play each other's parts was a deliberate tactic to keep us guessing is lost to the mists of time. I wouldn't bet against it though.

Unusually, Marc takes a lead vocal on the refrain, which could explain why Mark was less than enthusiastic about the song in hindsight. It could also have been the comparatively trivial nature of the lyric as a whole. Either way, he refused to include it on the 2005 re-issue of *Hex*, despite it being one of only three singles released by the *Hex* line-up and thus an obvious, not to say essential, addition.

The lyric shows Mark at his most schizophrenic – he takes the part of both the person being criticised and the one dishing out the disparagement, so the song ends up as an argument with himself. Though the first break is more generally directed at fashion obsessives, the bulk of the lyric takes the form of an imaginary conversation between Mark and the rest of the group, which explains Marc's prominent role. Semi-serious critiques of what we ate and what we chose to wear were fairly commonplace at the time,[124] and the answer to the question 'Do you know what you look like?' is printed on the back of the sleeve – 'These boys

[123] The Iceland recording has never come to light, as far as I'm aware.

[124] The aforementioned 'get your suits off, get your jeans on' line was added to the Peel version of 'C'n'C' when Marc and Craig turned up both wearing suits they'd picked up in a charity shop. 'Oh Brother's 'Your D-Jacket's a mess' was a (well deserved) snipe at the donkey jacket I wore throughout the early eighties, and 'Smile's 'tight faded male arse' was a reference to Karl's somewhat distressed black canvas jeans. They memorably split right the down middle on the first date of the 1981 European tour, and as they were the only kecks he had with him (and his predilection for going commando) he had to hide in the dressing room while the driver's wife sewed them up. Rather her than me.

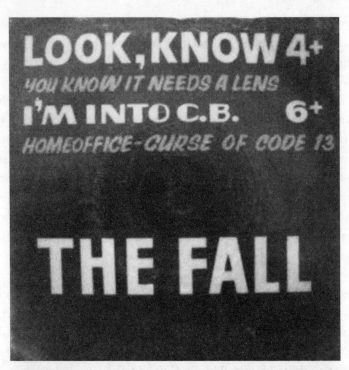

LOOK, KNOW 4+
YOU KNOW IT NEEDS A LENS
I'M INTO C.B. **6+**
HOMEOFFICE-CURSE OF CODE 13

THE FALL

ERA004

From the people who brought you ÷

'HORROR - SOUL":
'H------ SK--' :

```
media bag sez - 'y'know'
picker hit distrib. with nose for it sez - 'y'know'
it's a nasty business but - 'y'know'
radio group I comma View voice sez - 'Y'know,y'know,y'know y'know'
  Clear your mind of everything except the game.

HE was the first one to wear a harlequin type jacket and go to a club;
and SHE has a general policy of not being seen dead in a pub
straight leg jeans when she goes out,there's a microbe attached to their
brains which itches and gives a morning shout: Do y'know what you look like
before you go out.All fashions are Filched off faggots,then,TWO CR MCRE
YEARS LATER.....
-----------------------------------
PERFCRMED BY THE FALL
 incl. M.Riley-Vocal
       K.Carroll-keybds
       F.McCaffrey-bottles,wheels.
```

KAMERA RECORDS
DISTRIBUTED BY STAGE 1 RECORDS

These boys obviously do not

WARNING: (S) ADVOCATE YOUR DOCTOR
— MOST CAMERAS DON'T GIVE CANCER.

obviously do not'. Mark was fully aware that such criticisms were easy enough to direct back at him, which is why in the lyric you're never sure which voice is his. As the lyric evolved there were some changes to disguise this – the Peel version's 'That's why you messed up the interview' is changed to 'everything you do' on the single.

Though certainly not as polarising as the material that became *Room To Live*, 'Look, Know' remains one of the less-loved tracks by The Fall's *Hex* iteration. Certainly its writers were never entirely thrilled with it. As well as Mark's previously documented attempt to strike it from the record books, Steve was less than happy with the final recording.

Steve Hanley: I never imagined it to be like this, though. All bass and a bit of tinkly keyboards most of the way through. If it was up to me, there'd be more guitar. I'm thinking along the lines of Dexys-type soul with a brass section. But there isn't one.

As they were both recorded as part of the album sessions, the decision to leave 'I'm Into C.B' and 'Look, Know' off *Hex Enduction Hour* could be seen as credible evidence that Mark had an overriding theme in mind for the LP. It seems neither song was sufficiently preoccupied to justify a place on such a brooding album. The protagonist of 'I'm Into C.B.' is treated almost affectionately, and the criticisms inherent in the lyric of 'Look, Know' seem like mild irritation compared to 'Hey there fuck face' or 'subculture art-dealer jerk-off'. When something really pissed Mark off, you knew about it.

[SIDE ONE: TRACK 6] **Winter (Hostel Maxi)**
[SIDE TWO: TRACK 1] **Winter 2**

Words: Smith **Music:** Scanlon/Smith
(Smith/Scanlan)

Smith vocal; *Riley* keyboards; *Scanlon* guitar, vocal; *Hanley (S)* bass;
Hanley (P) guitar; *Burns* drums

First played live: 15th January 1981, Rafters, Manchester

Recorded: December 1981, studio, Regal Cinema, Hitchin

Producer: Richard Mazda. **Engineer:** Tony J. Sutcliffe

Released: 8th March 1982

RESPECT-INDUCING-HYPHEN

Steve Hanley: 'Winter' was, again, in that rehearsal room on Bury New Road bashing it out. Mark wasn't there most of the time. It's amazing we used to do this stuff without ever talking about it. We wouldn't sit in the pub saying 'I really like that riff' or 'what about a bridge?' – we've been in bands since with people who would rattle on for days about it if you'd let them.

Though Mark frequently dismissed musicians – particularly those in his immediate vicinity – as a breed of people who couldn't see the world beyond their instrument, none of the members of The Fall were remotely interested in discussing the finer points of musicality. And even if we had been, we didn't have the language to express it anyway.

Steve Hanley: You couldn't talk to Craig about chords, it would be all 'well I put my finger there, and this one there'.

Marc Riley: I've always said, if you were to throw us into a cabaret band and ask us to do 'Johnny B. Goode' in 'B' we'd have to say 'I haven't got a clue what you're talking about, I'm going home', but somehow we generated sounds that nobody else has. I'm more traditional than anybody, but Craig, he was making it up as he went along. But we had no tuition whatsoever, and we weren't even that intuitive to begin with. That was one big argument I had with Mark, early on, him and Kay were going on about us not being consistent. I said, 'We're not session musicians, we're not reliable, we're not classically trained. We don't know what we're doing.'

Steve Hanley: Mark would have hated using session musicians. It was an impossible ask – don't make mistakes but don't get too professional.

If The Fall in 1981 were of a mind to discuss the musicality of their songs, it's doubtful they'd start with this one, as it's built round a single note. Which isn't to say there aren't interesting things going on. Though it continues throughout the song, everyone veers from the root for extended periods, even me.[125]

By far the most striking example of Mark's singular vision is his decision to have Karl and Steve redo their respective parts against the original guitars and keyboards. He made out that their performances weren't strong enough, and though his typically surreal explanations as to why failed to convince anyone else, he obviously got his way. Instead of leaving the original drum track in and having Karl and Steve follow it, he wiped the whole rhythm section so they just had to try to keep up. There was no click track, of course, so keeping in time over the course of nine minutes was impossible – but Mark wasn't concerned about that. Karl and Steve reluctantly followed Mark's direction, against their better judgement, and their re-recording added something that no one but he knew the song needed. Like much of the album, the resulting track plays with the whole concept of keeping time. The rhythm section stays more-or-less in time with the rest of us for the first two-thirds of their re-recording, meaning that what later became the 'Hostel Maxi' section sounds relatively coherent. Midway through 'Part 2' it slips its moorings and lurches drunkenly away from the rest of the band till it's impossible to work out who's playing along with who. This deliberate use of the recording studio to craft something that was impossible for a band to recreate onstage (not that we were ever likely to try) was most unusual for The Fall, and it gives the lie to the accepted narrative that *Hex* was a glorified live recording. Everyone except Mark thought it was a terrible idea, but the timeslip brilliantly mirrors his lyric's blatant disregard for the conventions of linear time.

---

[125] With Marc playing keys his guitar was going spare, so that was what I played. As Craig rather unkindly put it, 'You were just grateful for the gig. Paul Hanley – spoons and violin, though we later wiped the spoons track.' Cheers Craig.

Marc Riley: We need to give Mark some credit there. He turned something that was quite straightforward into 'what the fuck's going on here?' like when you see the demon's face in *The Exorcist*. He did a similar thing with 'Spectre Vs. Rector', where half of the song is recorded on cassette.

The reference to *The Exorcist* is particularly apt, as both film and song ostensibly concern possession – as does 'Spector Vs, Rector', as it happens – but as with many of Mark's best lyrics, it's important not to get bogged down in the meaning of every single line. Trying to make sense of his 'lights' system of brain function is a case in point – just when you think you understand what he's saying about the mad kid's idiot savant intelligence he throws in the bit about the science law and all logic falls away.

Craig Scanlon: I like Mark's random stuff. His sparser stuff is his best, it really does fire the imagination. I don't need to hear him say 'I'm not from Bury' or 'I'm fifty years old'. I prefer when he's discrete and mysterious. 'Entrances uncovered, street signs you never saw' – what a brilliant line. Lyrically he was amazing. He really did break new ground, that people would try and copy, but it was impossible. Though you can do a good pastiche job by picking up the TV guide and reading out what's on on a Thursday.

According to the press release accompanying the album, '"Winter" is a tale concerning an "insane child" who is taken over by a spirit from the mind of a cooped-up alcoholic, and his ravaged viewpoints and theories.' There has been some debate as to the identity of the mad kid, and whether he was imaginary.

Craig Scanlon: I always thought the mad kid was Mark. I imagine he was a very *Kes*-like figure as a child. He was always a contrarian, so I can imagine him growing up that way. But I never felt the need to ask Mark about his lyrics – it would be like him asking me what that guitar line meant or how do you feel about that chord.

According to Karl at the time, the mad kid was a real person, and on one occasion he did offer to fight Mark and Karl as they passed him in the street. It's also interesting to note Martin Bramah's recollection of the first time he met Karl himself:

Martin Bramah: I first met Karl Burns on the street. He had this picture of Hitler and two of his henchmen and one had a ring round his head and Karl was insisting this was his father. That was my first meeting with Karl Burns, this mad kid claiming his dad was a Nazi.

But even if he did exist, the mad kid still became a figment of imagination as soon as Mark began putting pen to paper. The whole song appears to be an exercise in building an imaginary universe from the most mundane of observations. Where most of us would see a troubled boy on his way home from a party, Mark sees a child possessed. He envisions what's obviously a pirate's hat as 'a black cardboard Archbishop's hat with a green-fuzz skull and crossbones'. And while we're at it, do birds ever look like krakens? This ability to place such unusual imagery alongside a line as tinged with regret as 'I just looked round and my youth it was sold' is what made Mark E. Smith unique. It's also what makes speculation about his lyrical preoccupations so rewarding, even if we'll never know exactly what he was talking about. Because sometimes he didn't either.

Quality Nazi Pressing!

Richard Mazda: As a producer my job was almost to wrangle people's disjointed thoughts. My approach was to immerse myself in the feeling of the band, take on their attitude, interpret that and seek a common sound. That way I could give the band something they didn't know they were capable of.

The sound of *Hex Enduction Hour* was, by and large, set before a note was ever played. Of the two songs that hadn't been played live, 'Mere Pseud Mag. Ed.' had at least been fully rehearsed, and 'And This Day' was so random that it was impossible to finesse anyway. So, highly unusually, the group was ready to record *everything*. Mark, of course, had a few tricks to stop us getting too comfortable, but we managed the balancing act between naive exuberance and careful preparation pretty well. Combined with Richard's stated desire to capture the band's live sound, this made the production a fairly straightforward affair.

The album was mixed during the same Hitchin session, much of it as we went along – post-production was kept to a minimum. It certainly didn't take long – the songs recorded on the stage were pretty much left as-is, and even the studio ones had little in the way of manipulation or sonic enhancement. There were, of course, two significant pieces of editing required. While these were both primarily done to make the album exactly an hour long, it's difficult to argue that 'And This Day' isn't a better track for being trimmed of fifteen extraneous minutes. Similarly 'Winter's transformation from one to two songs adds an element of mystery that wasn't there previously. Quite when Mark got the idea to make *Hex* an hour is unknown, but once he had it he wasn't going to be dissuaded, even when it became clear that such a long single album was going to be difficult to manufacture.

Richard Mazda: The album had to be mastered in Germany because no one in the UK would touch it, even Porky Primecut.[126] They said that because it was an hour long the lathe would make the walls of the grooves so thin they would collapse, and the record would be constantly jumping. But there was a Telefunken facility in Hamburg that was used to pressing classical records which were often much longer than normal rock albums, so they agreed to do it.[127] I went out there to oversee the cut.

There were four or five friendly German guys present. They didn't really know The Fall, but they had heard of them. One of them asked 'Are they punk?' which was a difficult one to answer. The engineer explained that they liked to have the playback really loud, and I had no problem with that, so I told them to knock themselves out. They turned it up to eleven and hit 'play' and the first thing they heard was Mark screaming 'Who Makes The Nazis?' at the top his voice. They jumped out their fucking skins!

---

[126] George 'Porky' Peckham was the jovial scouser who was responsible for overseeing the 'cut' of master disks for many records of note from the late seventies to the nineties. A contemporary of The Beatles, he started out as a trainee disc-cutter at Apple. His catchphrase 'Any little messages?' will be familiar to anyone who made records during that period.

[127] It was actually the Teldec facility in Hamburg, which was originally a joint venture between Telefunken and Decca, hence the name.

2nd.-hand old U.S. ideas

Hex Enduction Hour is generally thought to be the album with the best Fall line-up, the strongest songs and the finest cover. As with the artwork of Smith's releases, this is a cover which comes at you from every angle with no consideration for conventional structure. It makes no sense, covered with abstract handwritten thoughts in cheap ink, commands heavily scratched and stated like a doodle by a deranged dictator. Its homemade aesthetic is confirmed by a badly set Letraset title, and a torn piece of unrecognisable painting.

Grant Scott in Barry Miles's *The Greatest Album Covers of All Time*

At this point in The Fall's career, Smith has acknowledged that there was an overabundance of words within The Fall's sound and *Hex Enduction Hour* bears out this assertion with phrases erupting chaotically onto the surface of the cover ... This multiplicity of voices reflects *Hex Enduction Hour*'s musical content: apparently structureless, repeated chaotic interruptions marked by sudden shifts in tone.

Paul Wilson, 'Language scraps – Mark E. Smith's Handwriting and Typography of The Fall'

The album sleeve, which was so foreign to what were then the conventions of sleeve design that HMV would only stock it with its reverse side facing forward, was the perfect visual analogue for the contents. The sleeve was more than that, actually; its spidery scrabble of slogans, scrawled notes and photographs was a part of the album rather than a mere illustrative envelope in which it was contained.

Mark Fisher, 'Memorex for the Krakens – The Fall's pulp modernism'

I like the cover to reflect what's inside.
Mark E. Smith

One of the few artists that Mark consistently cited as an influence, artist and writer Percy[128] Wyndham Lewis, started the 'Vorticist' artistic movement in 1914. Heavily influenced by Cubism, Vorticism was an attempt to tie art to industrialisation. It sought to move away from the sentimentality that Wyndham Lewis thought had too much of an influence over late nineteenth century art and literature. Instead it 'emphasized the value of violence, energy and the machine'.[129]

Mark E. Smith: I'd never seen anything like it. I liked the way it was all pamphlets, and *Blast* – which was one of the best magazines ever made. Still is. He was into manifestos as art. Nobody comes out with anything like that now, do they? 'Fuck machinery!' 'Bless machinery!' it was good.

The similarity between Mark E. Smith's approach to publicity and that of Wyndham Lewis and the Vorticists has been noted many times. Clearly, it's not difficult to draw parallels between Mark admitting 'Whenever I say anything, I often think that the opposite is true as well' and Wyndham Lewis exhorting us to 'contradict yourself. In order to live, you must remain broken up.' And as Craig has pointed out, there's also more than a hint of Wyndham Lewis's delight in saying the unspeakable in 'The Classical's 'Where are the obligatory n★★★★★s'. A 1992 article on the *Frieze* website expands on the parallels even further:

> Smith's polemic continues to affront every notion of political correctness, his audience recognize that his contrariness is merely a facet of a far more complex, and engaging, world vision. The ability to provoke and doubt, simultaneously, has often been cited as being fundamental to great art [and] like Wyndham Lewis, Mark E. Smith

[128] He dropped the 'Percy' early on, unsurprisingly.
[129] Wyndham Lewis lost much of his enthusiasm for the machine age after serving on the Western Front in World War I and witnessing first-hand the true consequences of industrialised violence. As he told leading Futurist Tommaso Marinetti in 1937: 'You Wops insist too much on the Machine. You're always on about these driving-belts, you are always exploding about internal combustion. We've had machines here in England for a donkey's years. They're no novelty to us.' He even sounds like MES.

will suggest the existence of a conspiracy behind most manifestations of modern culture.

If Mark E. Smith modelled the worldview he saw fit to share with others on Wyndham Lewis, then it's entirely appropriate, if surprisingly on-the-nose, for him to model the sleeve of arguably his most important work on *Blast*.

Written mainly by Lewis, signed off by his fellow Vorticists, who included Ezra Pound, Edward Wadsworth and Malcolm Arbuthnot, and first published in 1914, *Blast: Review of the Great English Vortex* was Vorticism's manifesto. Its challenging, wilfully contrary and often hilarious lists of 'Blast' and 'Bless' was hugely influential – and from the typeface down, the first edition was a direct antecedent of the cover of *Hex Enduction Hour*.

Dr. Michael Nath, novelist and senior lecturer at University of Westminster, sees a further connection in Wyndham Lewis and Mark E. Smith's surprising originality:

Michael Nath: The main thing is that both the words in the *Blast* manifestos and in Mark Smith's lyrics are very similar in their magic – they take the reader/listener by surprise, because they're not attached in normal ways. And you do feel you're *listening* to *Blast,* as much as reading it, which applies to the *Hex* cover as well.

With their blatant disregard for the conventions of capitalisation, and playful juxtapositions of the meaningless and the pointed, many of the phrases on the front cover of *Hex Enduction Hour* would feel at home in *Blast* and vice-versa. Moreover the grammar of the back cover's 'explanations' of the songs is heavily influenced by the 'Manifesto' segment of *Blast*'s first issue, in both layout and language. If *Blast* made a virtue of its hurried-looking typography (though in reality it was anything but), then Mark went even further: the majority of *Hex*'s cover is rendered in his own free-hand. Paul Wilson noted that the switch from the *Blast*-referencing portion of the sleeve to the even more chaotic handwritten section was deliberate:

A sense of tension exists between the visual order of the design's top third and the collaged free-for-all of the other two-thirds. This ... seem[s] to be an attempt at marking out some kind of quiet(er) space, a pause or silence before the typographic deluge, the apotheosis of Mark Smith's handwritten cover design: an overload of aphorisms, visualized using a range of tools, approaches and styles.

Kamera's willingness to go along with that, in addition to agreeing to master an hour-long record against the prevailing wisdom, was one of the many reasons he felt so warmly towards them.

In August 2017, Mark was scheduled to perform 'Responding to a Rebel: Mark E. Smith Agent of Chaos', his 'personal response' to Wyndham Lewis's work, which would have consisted of readings and improvised music. This was part of 'Wyndham Lewis: Life, Art, War', an exhibition and events season at the Imperial War Museum. In the end he was too unwell to do it, but the fact that he was willing to contribute shows how highly he regarded Wyndham Lewis's work. There is one striking difference between the two writers however, as Mark himself has pointed out:

Mark E. Smith: I was talking to one woman about Wyndham Lewis and she went into this rant for about 20 minutes about how he was a fascist and all that. I was saying, 'Alright luv, we all know that. But at least he apologised for his mistakes.'

HEXEN School

Like everything else to do with *Hex Enduction Hour,* the title of the album is open to some degree of interpretation.

As well as openly sign-posting the magic within by including the word 'Hex' (which can mean both 'spell' and 'curse') Mark reinforced this by mis-spelling 'induction'[130] so that the title would also contain 'Hexen' (German for 'witches').

The word 'Hexen' got a song of its own a year later: 'Hexen Definitive', which repeats the phrase 'Hexen school', as seen in both English and German on the cover of *Hex Enduction Hour.* It also mentions 'Hexen Hour' and 'The hour of The Fall', which would point to the fact that *Hex*'s length was a deliberate signifier of Mark's message, just like the sleeve itself. So is the sixty-minute induction process intended to introduce the listener to the magic of The Fall, or to magic itself? Or both?

John Doran has posited that the album as a whole is actually a magic spell or occult ritual – citing the references to Colin Wilson's *Ritual in the Dark* and 'Jawbone and the Air-Rifle's 'cursed mandible' as evidence of the arcane rite therein. He's also suggested that 'Winter's 'entrances uncovered' is a play on the phrase 'entrancers uncovered'.

Kay has a different idea about the origins of the album's title, stemming from our trip to Iceland:

Kay Carroll: Einar took us way out and showed us this huge volcano, The Heck, which he said was 'the gateway to hell'. I never asked, because Mark's credo was 'what does it mean to you?' but *Heck's Enduction Hour* …?

They're both interesting theories, and both could be correct, though it's ultimately unprovable. But that's beside the point.

---

[130] A reference to the 'hypnotic induction process' mentioned in 'Just Step S'ways' and used as an acronym in 'Hip Priest'.

While most dissections of cited albums must content themselves with discussing the lyrics and the music, there's so much going on in *Hex Enduction Hour* that *everything* has to be taken into consideration. The typeface, the song credits, the running order, the title, even the length of the album can be cited as evidence of *something*. Given it's such a complete package, maybe Mark did mean it to be his final statement, to be analysed and pondered over for years to come. 'Full of strangeness, like a rich painting,' as the song goes.

Flabby Wings

The equipment The Fall used around the time *Hex* was recorded was, without exception, cheap and second hand. The group's attitude to instruments and amps was mostly unsentimental – unlike many bands none of the members had much of a predilection for amassing *gear* as a hobby in its own right. Because of this lackadaisical approach to hardware, some details of what we used are lost to the mists of time.

Marc Riley
Fender Stratocaster, bought from the Nightingales' Robert Lloyd – the case had 'This is a Prefect's Sten Gun' written on the inside. Lloyd had forgotten to remove his guitar strap, a lovely nubuck-leather one that had been signed by Link Wray, before making the sale. Marc eventually gave it him back the next time the two bands' paths crossed. Marc also had a Hofner Galaxie around the same time, but this may have been sold to pay for the Strat.

Elgam Snoopy electric piano – Elgam was an Italian company and Ennio Morricone used the Snoopy on several soundtracks. It only had three sounds: piano, harpsichord and spinet, which could be mixed together using the sliders. None of the sounds had much sustain, which meant Marc had to play as fast as he could with two fingers on the same key to achieve long notes (you can hear an example of this on 'New Face in Hell'). He purchased a CRB Elettronica Diamond 600 organ before *Hex*, which added a whole new dimension to his sound. It came in a striking shade of beige and had four voices, all of which were remarkably similar and Hammond-esque. One distinct advantage of the Diamond 600 image-wise was that it had its own legs and also had room for the Snoopy on top, which rendered Marc's ironing-board stand redundant.

Craig Scanlon

Hagstrom Futurama III. Made in Sweden in the mid-1960s and bought by Craig for £25 from A1 Repairs, Manchester. Craig customised it by chopping off the top arm for ease of left-handed playing, and hand-painting it with black gloss because he didn't like the rather fetching shade of red it came in. The publicity pictures of David Bowie circa 'Rebel Rebel' where he's sporting an eye patch will give you a glimpse of what it originally looked like. Craig had a Park combo amplifier (Park were Marshall's budget line).

Craig Scanlon: My favourite guitar. I didn't alter the pick-ups, i.e. turn them upside down, which I'm sure gave the bass/treble strings a different sound – I'm no guitar expert.

Steve Hanley

Fender Precision bass, unsurprisingly. The one he used on *Hex* was a lovely natural finish. At the time he was using an HH V-S BassAmp though a Park cab.

None of the group's guitarists used any effects pedals.

Karl Burns

Karl had sold his *Live at the Witch Trials* drum kit some time after originally leaving The Fall, and he used my kit for the dates when we played alternate nights. So when we went with the double drummer line-up he hired a green Pearl Export kit from Mamelok's on Deansgate and never returned it. Unusually, his kit had only one cymbal, an Avedis 18-inch crash/ride.[131] Toms were 14-inch and 16-inch respectively.

My kit wasn't really a kit at all. I had a matching Olympic 20-inch bass drum and 12-inch tom in pearl, that I bought off Paul Eastman, the drummer from The Sirens.[132] I also had an ancient

---

[131] Avedis (and you may be sensing a theme here) was the budget arm of Zildjian.

[132] The Sirens was Craig, Marc and Steve's pre-Fall group, which featured Steve Murray, later of Fast Cars, on vocals. Their repertoire included The Velvet Underground's 'I'm Waiting for the Man' and 'I'm Down' by The Beatles. The Sirens played just one gig, on the 11th January 1978 at Pips in Manchester.

Premier snare that was so rusted it wouldn't let you release the snares.[133] I had to borrow a floor tom off the group Fashion for my first gig with The Fall, but I was bought a Rogers 16-inch floor tom when I became an official member. I had two cymbals (flash!), which I presume were Avedis as well. I do know that neither of them cost very much, and that one of them eventually split rather badly.[134]

Karl, Craig and Steve's equipment, as described above, was stolen from our van on Thursday 1st November 1984, after a gig at the New Ocean Club, Cardiff. Also taken was the new drum kit I had acquired when we signed to Beggars Banquet. I only managed one more gig than the kit – I left The Fall the next day.[135] Marc took his guitars and keyboards with him when he exited the group, but the Snoopy and the Diamond 600 were left in the cellar of his flat in Sale when he moved on. I told you we were unsentimental.

[133] I replaced this with a Yamaha snare – with a fully-functioning snare release – shortly after we recorded *Hex Enduction Hour*. I took advantage of this new string to my bow on 'Wings' and 'Garden', which are both played with the snares off. You're learning some good stuff here, aren't you?

[134] It sounded great when it first split, a bit like the syndrum on 'She's Lost Control'. Didn't sound so good when it fell in half, mind.

[135] Mark kept a lid on his fury at the gear being stolen long enough for us to play the final date of the tour then went absolutely ballistic, literally waving a big stick around and reminding me he could sack me whenever he felt like it. I decided to save him the trouble.

he had been frightened of himself far too much. Now, as he paced the
creaking boards, this realisation filtered into his psyche and for the
first time he understood the words 'gratitude' 'sympathy' and 'big
personality face'. Their dictionary meanings were intended to oppress,
especially the last two. Gratitude was still useful in that it could
mean the random forces of nature working for his good, and him seeing
that. Paganism. He'd been very close to becoming ex-funny man celebrity.
He needed a good hour at the Hexen school, a word mutant of two languages
he'd grasped from thin air.

HEX ENDUCTION HOUR

× New l.p. !

THE FALL

1ST: HEXEN-BILE, HEXEN CURSES

THE SCOURGE OF 'ROSSO-ROSSO'

'HEX Enduction Hour' is official new Fall product on Kamera
Records, and in the groups opinion their most concentrated work to date.
And maybe it will. It is packed with typical Fall appreciation of the
good things in life, plus the usual niggly, annoying, BITTY observations
that keep the group well away from the over exposed minds of our time.

'There is no culture is my brag' _ 'The Classical'

THE LITTLE THINGS JOIN UP

TO MAKE:

Track listing:

Side a. The Classical-Jawbone & The Air-Rifle-Hip Priest-Fortress, Deer
         Park-Mere Pseud Mag. Ed-Winter(Hostel-Maxi)

Side b: Winter 2 -Just Step S'Ways-Who Makes the Nazis?-Iceland-And This
         Day.
personnel same as last 45 release 'Lie-Dream Of A Casino Soul'

The first 50 mins of the l.p. are songs honed in from the last tours The
Fall have performed, the first side songs of comment and attitude, the 2nd
side especially last 2 tracks 'Iceland' and 'And This Day', intends to
intimidate the listener into the Fall's intelligence thru noise waves(!)
'And This Day' was savagely and randomly edited to produce new lyrics &
impossible notes. Satirical, humourous element of past Fall work v. underplayed
because 1. they've wrung it dry 2. t.v. is riddled now with liquidified
'satire' in most cases inferior to what the 'satirists' are trying to takea
da piss out of.

        BLAST First (from politeness) ENGLAND
                                              -W.Lewis 1914

WARNING: THERE ARE NO BLONDE BIRDS ON THE COVER OR IN THE RECORD.

                                          P.T.O.

PART III
W/M.S. – BIG PERSONALITY FACE

TEXT EXCERPT FROM: AND THIS DAY

> And this day no matter what and never or who fills baskets or
> who's just there, the whole earth shudders
> You show me the bloody poor bores/The surroundings are screaming on
> the roads,so you even mistrust your own feelings
> And this day,the old feelings came back;
> Big basket full s'-park s'-mart
> Everywhere just no fucking respite for us here,John kidder
> And this day,it will soon heal up.

'Winter' is a tale concerning an insane child who is taken over by a
spirit from the mind of a cooped-up alcoholic,and his ravaged viewpoints
and theories.An earlier version went into the 'Clang' process of speech,
whereby the sufferer during speech makes sentences containg similar sounding words.   MX

Hex Enduction Hour was recorded in an empty cinema,a studio adjacent to
it,and 'Hip Priest' was recorded in a studio made of lava(:)

Production: Richard Mazda/Grant Cunliffe/Mark E. Smith

The Sign OF Quality

BIG.   P.   You know it needs a
                              lens.

next single announcement:
   45 rpm   SIDE A: 'LOOK,KNOW'
              SIDE B: 'I'M INTO C.B.'

side A is a new version of a fairly old song recorded using the same
        technique as 'And This Day'.Lyric is a schizo rant,spawned in
        the U.S., where many groups are becoming male go-go dancers

side B: Is a comment on the weedy Home Office Sanctioned LIBERACE-ISM
        of U.K. band transmissions.
                                          out terminal Mar.82

Any mail should be sent to: The Fall c/o V.M. 284 Pentonville Rd.
                                                   London N.

please do not expect a reply,as The Fall are not a condescending French
resistance type group nor do they have warehouses packed with info kits
on themselves.Thankyou.

                              M.E.S. Mar 82

Spite does not enter into this

> *Hex Enduction Hour*, the first of The Fall's two long-players last year, was the most violent and uncompromising record of 1982. Like a gutterful of despair-sodden dregs, it sprayed out the sludge in the sources of our terrible malaise – lies, stupidity and selfish greed – and proceeded to douse them all further in a soup of amplified retching and cut-up half-sense.
>
> Much like any Fall record, in fact, except that Smith's group had crept almost unnoticed to a level of sophistication that challenged the given precepts of 'The Fall' as we had known them. The kind of music that was being played on 'The Classical' or the absolutely withering 'And This Day' had all the tension of skilled improvised music married to an unflinching grasp of form: tyrannical, claustrophobic, it smelt of decay and renewal in exact counterbalance.
>
> **Richard Cook, 'The Curse of The Fall'**
> ***NME*, 15th January 1983**

'Uncompromising' is probably the key word here. In order to ensure that *Hex Enduction Hour* met his expectations, Mark had refused to play ball with Rough Trade, with the rest of his group, with the rules of rock music, with accepted ideas of what a record sleeve should look like, and even with how much music you can fit on a single long player. We can only be grateful for that. If we're examining what makes a good album an *important* album, then surely such clarity of vision is a key factor. That's not to say *Hex* belongs, in any way, to Mark alone – he had a hand in the music of 'Mere Pseud Mag. Ed.', 'Deer Park' and 'Who Makes The Nazis?', but nothing else. But the fact that he had such a clear idea of what he wanted elevates *Hex* above many other Fall LPs, particularly the ones where he was content just to record enough material to justify a release.

As Brian Edge noted in *Paintwork — A Portrait of The Fall*:

> This was their last truly quantum leap: after *Hex* The Fall
> always seemed to know what they were doing, to be aware
> of the fact that they were The Fall.

This is borne out by the fact that, somewhat unexpectedly, contemporary reviews of *Hex Enduction Hour* were overwhelmingly favourable.

Writing in the *NME*, Richard Cook was evidently so taken with the album that he was moved to forgo punctuation: 'There is no other group to harness rock's primal raw-nerved energy with such an intuitive sense of destructuralisation that extends from Smith's sawn-off lyrics and uncannily provocative vocals through the inspired rule-breaking in the actual playing to the stubbornly anti-resonant production.' He was particularly impressed with the way The Fall had progressed since their previous releases, noting that '*Hex Enduction Hour* is sixty minutes of The Fall with all their previous incarnations toughened to a bitterly frightening degree. Though it's easy to charge them with being infuriatingly obtuse in the past it is now clear that Smith has disciplined the progress of his group with an iron logic. Listening to *Hex* is as biliously purgatorial as listening to *Dragnet* was in 1979, but the steps forward are tangible.'

Over in *Sounds*, Edwin Pouncey (who could be accused of having a conflict of interests, having designed the sleeve of our previous single) was convinced that '*Hex Enduction Hour* is the furthest adventure The Fall have ever embarked upon, one that absorbs and holds the listener in a grip of iron. It is also more importantly The Fall's finest hour.'

Colin Irwin in *Melody Maker* was sufficiently moved to reveal that 'I love this LP. It's incredibly exciting and utterly compelling', though he was at something of a loss to explain why. 'I doubt that any Fall fan could coherently describe what captivates them so. The challenge? The nerve? A furious charisma which offers real delusions that *Hex Enduction Hour* is exploding in front of me as I play it? The knowledge that alongside The Fall, almost every other band in the world seems absurdly trivial?'

For the *NME* at least, the album quickly became part of the musical firmament. When Echo & The Bunnymen released *Porcupine* in February 1983, both Barney Hoskyns's review and Richard Cook's subsequent interview with the group were moved to compare the album to *Hex*. Hoskyns remarked that '[*Porcupine*]'s final exhausted throes are as draining (and as moving) as the bleakest moments of *Hex Enduction Hour* but devoid of The Fall's humour', while Cook thought that it had a 'welter of personal doubt and disquiet which drives through the most radical investigation of sound this side of *Hex Enduction Hour*'.

The *NME*'s 1982 reviews of Cabaret Voltaire's *2X45* and Siouxsie and the Banshees' *A Kiss in the Dream House* also used The Fall as a touchstone:

> Like The Fall – a group whose single-mindedness CV have much in common with – Voltaire have worked at definition and detail.

> The Banshees' discipline of their progress is what has allowed them to move on: as with Smith and The Fall, the only other group of their era to have retained their dignity.[136]

Such positive opinion, and an accompanying sense that The Fall were a now a benchmark by which contemporary post-punk bands were judged, had a not-entirely expected effect on Mark, and consequently the group as a whole. As soon became clear, Mark wasn't entirely comfortable with the approbation, as Mick Middles has pointed out:

> [*Hex*] was the record which saw the band promoted, as it were, with gates opened for a flood of new faces. In short, they no longer seemed like our local band, no doubt much to Mark's delight. What he hadn't realised, though, was that the album would be deemed so accessible; bizarrely, one almost sensed his disappointment at the largely supportive reviews. It was, after all, a deliberate attempt to step away from the gawdy pop scramble.

---

[136] Both these reviews were written by Richard Cook. He really liked *Hex Enduction Hour*, didn't he?

Smith and Scanlan in typical hi-tech habitat.   Pic: Anton Corbijn.

THESE FALLISH THINGS

THE FALL

Hex Enduction Hour (Kamera)

"Everyone gets too serious about The Fall."
Mark E Smith, November 1981

LET'S GET serious. Let's see The Fall as the scabrous prowlers of the grey area between rackety garage playing the guilty code of songwriting mechanics, chords and tunes and stuff like that. Or let's see them as the first and only anti-rock rock group fuelled on an invective indiscriminate in its attack on the buttresses of the machine. Or as the ashen, hungry spectres in the phantom zone of prole art.

Or, more realistically, as none of these. The Fall have never been what they seem. They have become an apotheosis of alien abstraction. Outside of the Magic Band — whose other-worldly imaginings of rock's coarsest R&B roots question any categorisation anyway — there is no other group to harness rock's primal raw-nerved energy with such an intuitive sense of destructuralisation that extends from Smith's sawn-off lyrics and uncannily provocative vocals through the inspired rule-breaking in the actual playing to the stubbornly anti-resonant production. Hence tags like 'northern rockabilly' or 'modern folk'. Only The Fall, among English groups, manipulate such a recognisable, repetitive rock primer to such desperate extremes. The Fall's return to an older order is despised partly because its insularity cannot be breached.

'Hex Enduction Hour' is sixty minutes of The Fall with all their previous incarnations toughened to a bitterly frightening degree. Though it's easy to charge them with being infuriatingly obtuse in the past it is now clear that Smith has disciplined the progress of his group with an iron logic. Listening to 'Hex' is as biliously purgatorial as listening to 'Dragnet' was in 1979, but the steps forward are tangible. The advances eked out over the series of 45s and LPs between the two poles — principally, a strengthening of studio sound without resorting to glamourisation and the diversification of the internal combustion peculiar to a Fall tune when it lurches into life — were imparted like a gradual rediscovery of turmoil: until 'Slates' and 'Fantastic Life' presented a group of enormous intensity. But still one resolutely attuned to the spirit of a primitive piece like 'It's The New Thing'.

More than ever, 'Hex' perpetrates the idea of The Fall blurred into a single, rabidly ugly, threshing rock hobgoblin. Smith's vocals are habitually decentralised and emerge like a loudhailer harangue from a fog of guitar scratch that unscrambles into any necessary riff as if by magic. The only new clarity is in the two-drum base which literally flays most of these — songs.

Or clammy dissertations, spewed outrages, acrid monologues . . . Mark Smith's latest chain of thought really makes no concession to the accessibility he mentioned the record would have last year. When Smith's scabbed commentary is decipherable only odd phrases come through, often shown in the scrawled montage on the cover: it is enough that his scumhouse rhetoric is intact, perhaps. Only 'Hip Priest', a self-denial of deification laden with curmudgeonly sarcasm, seems at all clear.

What is most vital is the assertion of the other players. Whereas previous Fall LPs always drew the ear straight to that incomparably scurvied voice, 'Hex' makes Smith take his place beside the severe concentration of the others. 'Winter' and 'Winter 2' fade in and out, formless, ragged rambles that sound like a backing track which runs endlessly through their heads, forever recycled with a ghastly compulsion. Beside these, the insolent, bullet-hard expression of 'Jawbone And The Air-Rifle' or 'Fortress/Deer Park' seems almost a perversion; just as the closing ten minutes of 'And This Day', a sick sea of reddled fuzzbox assault and a blubbering drumbeat that's a second cousin to 'Pena', reassures us of that bloody-mindedness.

As for the drear, muted 'Hip Priest' and 'Who Makes The Nazis?', or the improvised-in-Reykjavik ghostworld of 'Iceland', The Fall approach such sparer atmospherics with the same revealing sureness.

The dilemma now would seem to be where Smith can take them next, before diminishing returns eventually set in. Deprived of their audience — the blighted proletariat Smith's work draws on are too busy buying Jam records to bother with The Fall — their problem lies in how to evolve further a music which has already turned in on itself. Because Mark Smith is determined to play rock music (does a secret rocky reactionary sometimes squirm behind those pullovers? Remember 'Lie Dream Of A Casino Soul' or "For God's sake don't start improvising?") of the most elemental kind The Fall have sealed their isolation: they can never be an influence because nobody can progress on what they have done except The Fall themselves.

Either way, what they have done on 'Hex Enduction Hour' is create their masterpiece to date. Seriously.

Richard Cook

In fact Mark was so uncomfortable with the group being feted by the UK inkies that he took steps to ensure the same wouldn't happen again, including openly mocking the rest of the group's apparent delight at *Hex*'s popularity.

Mark E. Smith: (At Leicester Polytechnic, 24th March 1982): Sorry the boys are a bit ropey tonight, but they believe everything they read about themselves, you know what I mean? Yeah, right.

His next move was to take the group as far 'away from the gaudy pop scramble' as it's possible to get. He was determined that The Fall's next release wouldn't be judged as a pale imitation or an inferior attempt at a follow up to *Hex Enduction Hour*. As Richard Cook had noted in his review of *Hex* for the *NME:*

> The dilemma now would seem to be where Smith can take them next, before diminishing returns eventually set in.

It wasn't a dilemma that overly troubled Mark. In order to avoid any possibility that The Fall's next album could be judged as a second-rate version of *Hex Enduction Hour*, Smith made *Room To Live (Undilutable Slang Truth)* its polar opposite. It was short where *Hex* was long; it was un-premeditated and deliberately un-prepared where *Hex* was planned and coherent; and instead of making the most of the group's six-piece synergy, *Room To Live* only featured the whole group on two of its seven tracks.

It was recorded at John Brierley's Cargo studios in Rochdale, which was close enough for everyone to go home at the end of each session. For Mark, this was advantageous as it meant he could instruct Paul, our driver, not to pick certain people up on some days.[137] On one occasion, the first Steve and I knew about Marc having the day off was when Paul turned left out of our drive instead of going straight on to his house. It didn't make for the easiest of atmospheres.

[137] Paul McCaffrey. He got a credit (bottles, wheels) on the back of the 'Look, Know' sleeve.

Marc Riley: *Room To Live* was Mark's attempt to split me and Steve up, to get me out of the group. He definitely had some masterplan, even if it was only sabotage.

It was obvious that Craig, Marc, Steve and I were almost a band within a band, a Catholic cabal who hung around together all the time – 'the Jesuits' was one of Mark's collective names for us. Sometimes Karl would be with us, sometimes he would be with Mark. But there was always a distinction between the two factions. And this gave us some collective bargaining power ('mick slyness') that Mark wasn't always entirely happy with.

'Joker Hysterical Face' is the only song on *Room To Live* to feature the whole group with Karl and me both playing drums, and as such it's the most *Hex*-like of the album's seven songs. It was mainly composed by Marc and is the only song on the album to feature him on guitar. Given how well it succeeds, it's obvious that Mark's reasons for shaking up the status quo had little to do with the formula becoming stale. It was supposedly written about Mark's downstairs neighbours who liked to play Abba and Roberta Flack records at full volume. The outro quotes Flack's hit 'The First Time Ever I Saw Your Face', as written by Mark's fellow Salfordian Ewan MacColl.

'Solicitor in Studio' also featured the whole band, but this time Karl played second bass. Like 'Joker Hysterical Face' it had been a live staple for quite some time, and had a fully realised arrangement.

Craig Scanlon: That was one of mine – I love the way it breaks down. Marc's keyboards were brilliant, and Karl's bass was great.

Unlike most of *Room To Live*, it also had a discernible chorus. Not that that mattered when we were invited to play over the end credits of *Granada Reports*, the North-West regional magazine programme that often-featured Tony Wilson. The programme ended before we got anywhere near the chorus.

The rest of the songs on *Room To Live* were all worked up in the studio. For some of the songs Mark engaged Arthur Kadmon, the guitarist in Manchester band Ludus, to add guitar. The first the rest of us knew of this was when we arrived expecting a normal day's recording.

Marc Riley: I turned up when Arthur Kadmon was playing guitar, and bless him, he felt terrible. He really freaked out.

Strangely, Kadmon hadn't brought anything with him to play. Sensing everyone's discomfort, he refused to use Marc's guitar or tuner and was forced to use a cheap guitar that had been left in the studio at some time in the past which steadfastly defied his efforts to tune it by ear. Nonetheless, his hastily improvised and surprisingly melodic guitar can be heard on 'Room To Live' and 'Hard Life in the Country', though Kadmon was only given a matter of minutes (and one run through) to add his parts. Both songs also featured Craig on guitar. If, as Marc recalls, he was there at the same time as Kadmon, this means he must have been present when the stand-in guitarist effectively took his position in the band. In the end 'Room To Live' was vastly improved once the whole band got hold of it after the album was complete. Unsurprisingly, given how sparse it was, 'Hard Life in the Country' stayed pretty much the same.

'Marquis Cha-Cha', which consisted of a brilliant Falklands War-based satire set to a suitably South-American dance shuffle (though a tango would have been more appropriate than a cha-cha-chá) is perhaps the most obvious victim of Mark's new approach.

Craig Scanlon: We weren't aware of the subterfuge, me and Marc were told we were all having the day off. It was a terrible way to treat people.

Neither Marc nor Craig (nor Arthur Kadmon) appeared on the track, and the first time the 'song', which consisted of Karl's drum part, Marks vocal and a tentative bassline, was presented to Steve and me was the day it was recorded. What's more the guitar, which should have acted as the bedrock of the song, was overdubbed afterwards by Karl. Nevertheless, Mark was happy to present a tentative run through, with a succession of timing errors and fluffs, as the finished article.[138]

Craig Scanlon: 'Marquis Cha-Cha' was a brilliant concept, but it was completely half-baked.

One by-product of Mark's insistence on developing five brand new songs in Cargo was that a number of other, and arguably better, songs which had also been regularly part of the group's live set prior to entering the studio, went unrecorded, some forever.

'The Man Whose Head Expanded' and 'Wings' were recorded later and released as a single and B-side respectively; 'Tempo House' and 'Hexen Definitive' were included on 1983's *Perverted By Language* album. 'Draygo's Guilt' eventually saw the light of day, some four-and-a-half years after its live debut, on 1984's *Call for Escape Route* EP. Two other songs which were regularly played live in 1982, 'Session Musician' and 'Backdrop', were never recorded, though they did both appear on official live albums.[139]

The review of *Room To Live (Undilutable Slang Truth)* by Amrik Rai in the *NME* was the first to articulate what later became the general consensus:

> Where *Hex Enduction Hour* was a collection of immaculately neat, complete, shrink-wrapped and bouncy classics, *Room To Live* is scarcely more substantial than a tawdry collection of scantily-clad doodles.

---

[138] Though Steve says in *The Big Midweek* that 'Marquis Cha-Cha' only features him, Karl and Mark, I am on there, providing the rim shots on the verse and the snare on the intro/break. (Karl plays the hi-hats, bass drum and timbale, which was actually his snare with snares off.) So the timing issues are as much my fault as anyone else's. For an idea of what the song sounded like when it had been fully learned, arranged and rehearsed, see the version on *Fall in a Hole* or the recording made for Radio 1's *Saturday Live* in 1984.
[139] There was also 'Surrogate Mirage' which we only ever played a couple of times, for some reason. It featured a fully-fleshed out, if enigmatic, lyric, paired with a suitably haunting tune. Why it was so unceremoniously ditched is anyone's guess.

Of course Mark could then claim that anyone who was disappointed with the way *Room To Live* was put together was merely demonstrating their inability to adapt and move on as quickly as he could. And this was true of journalists, fans and the rest of his group alike. Just like when we attempted a kick-about in Mandley Park, Mark was always ready to move the goalposts no matter who told him it was a bad idea.

Mark E. Smith: I'm dead proud of that record. A good cleaning-out of the system. It got misinterpreted a lot. [...] I don't think there is anything wrong with it at all. I think, at the time, it was one of those albums that tended to stretch beyond the expectations of The Fall fans, but that has always been a Fall thing. It probably isn't the easiest Fall record to listen to, but that's partly its strength ... there's a lot of good stuff in there. [...] and I wanted ... to try and capture a rawness, to make a picture of the songs so they would stand up. That's what I tried to get into the group's heads by throwing in people who they'd never worked with before. I mean I played the same trick on the group as the people who bought the record really ... I like strong lyrics and it's pretty irrelevant whether it's jazz behind it or whatever. [...] I thought we were getting a bit restricted by *Hex*, it was so 'thought out', planned, and like, intensive. That's why I've shuffled round with the band, I didn't want the same sound reproduced twice. We've only used one drum set on here, a bit of an experiment, and I excluded some of the band from certain tracks, shuffled them round a bit, and used some outside musicians. All of The Fall are on the record, but not all of them on every track, which I did to keep with this 'instant' thing that we've had in the past – the far past! The band weren't even familiar with some of the songs, we just went in and did them which is how we always operated in the good old days! And I think it's served to stir them up a bit! I suppose I'm a contrary bastard – I like to do the opposite of what I've just done.

Opinion has become less scathing about *Room To Live* in the years following its release and even those critics who still dislike some aspects of it admire the way Mark refused to rest on his laurels. But it's hardly surprising it holds so little affection for those of us who played on it. After all, we weren't aware we needed 'stirring up' and, contrary to Mark's assertion, the band had never ever operated that way before.

Craig Scanlon: Mark always used to destroy when it was getting too popular, he was scared of that, he always wanted to be just under. I was never bothered about chart positions either.

Possibly coincidentally, *Room To Live* was the last release by The Fall on Kamera.

Mark E. Smith: Kay was the first one to realise that something was amiss at Kamera; that things weren't tallying up as they should. She had it right as well, as they went bust soon after. I was a bit gutted about that. They had the right idea there.

Chris Youle: The label went bust, probably because Eric and I were not fully committed to the direction the label was going. Steve had sold Human to Patrick Meehan at NEMS and part of the deal was that I would go with it, so we moved to Ecclestone Street in Victoria. NEMS had Black Sabbath but were no different to Rough Trade in my eyes, so it all ended in tears and I moved out. Kamera moved to Marylebone with Saul taking the lead in matters A&R. Unfortunately, his enthusiasm wasn't met with the financial returns needed to run the label. Saul went on to a great and successful career with Nude – a career which continues to this day. I continued managing Roger Chapman until 1992 when we split, and I left the music biz for good. I'm still friends with Saul and Steve Melhuish remains my best friend.

Mark E. Smith: We had to leave Kamera because we knew it was going down, it broke my heart. Kamera were like, Here y'are mate, what you're saying is fantastic. *Hex Enduction Hour* is brilliant, you're brilliant, here's a cheque. You play *Hex* to them, they go, Fuckin' brilliant, mate! Uriah Heep at its best! Only label I was upset to leave. [...It] meant that we had to fuck off back to Rough Trade, which I was very unhappy about. It felt like going back to a job that you'd confidently walked out of six months ago, telling everybody about the lucrative future that lay in wait; only to find yourself back there six months later, looking like a prize pillock.

As ever true to his word, Chris made sure the rights to The Fall's material reverted to the band. This enabled the release of the compilation album *Hip Priest and Kamerads* on Beggars Banquet offshoot Situation 2 in 1985.

Rather less coincidentally, *Room To Live* was also the last Fall release to feature Marc Riley. Between its recording in June 1982 and eventual release in October, the group completed a punishing schedule of live appearances, starting with an extensive tour of Australia and New Zealand. The various verbal and physical disagreements between Mark and Marc on the tour have been well documented, though much of the tension came from being away from home for so long. And if Mark had been willing they could probably have been resolved. Unfortunately, things didn't improve for December's tour of the UK, and if anything, Mark stepped up his constant and completely unjustified denigration of Marc's playing. It became increasingly clear that something would have to give, and to no one's real surprise Marc was sacked over the phone in December 1982. With that, the line-up that had written and recorded *Hex Enduction Hour* was no more.

EARN'D hexen-schule

Is *Hex* any good, some 37 years after its release?

Well, it's been regularly feted as a landmark album in the context of The Fall, and sometimes even in the wider context of pop/rock music as a whole. Quite why that is isn't immediately obvious. It wasn't the group's debut, it has little of the crossover pop sheen of *This Nation's Saving Grace*, and it sold far less at the time of its release than *Extricate*. It probably wasn't Mark E. Smith's favourite Fall album, and it definitely wasn't recorded by what he would regard as the group's best line-up. Musically it was neither rewardingly polished nor endearingly unrefined. Lyrically, it was sometimes uncomfortably brazen, even amongst the output of a man who made a career out of being willfully uncompromising.

Yet it has, and continues to be, the subject of many articles and think pieces in diverse and sometimes unexpected publications. As someone who was involved in its recording, it's almost alarming in 2019 to see *Hex* in Q magazine's '156 Most Influential Records Of All Time', alongside such seminal works as *Dark Side of the Moon* or *Low*. Certainly, at the time of its release, no one, including the group, would have predicted that, as the accompanying article by Stewart Lee makes clear:

> A repetitive, pulverising barrage of unpleasantness, briefly leavened by varying degrees of intensity, and vandalized by the incoherent hectoring of its horrible non-singing singer.[140]

As Simon Ford sees it, '*Hex Enduction Hour* brought out everything, everything that was great about The Fall', and writing for *Billboard* in 2018, Nathaniel Friedman was adamant that the 'barrage of unpleasantness' is actually the point:

[140] It's his favourite album.

This all-consuming ugliness is why some people find The Fall unlistenable. As one friend put it, 'I already feel hellish and anxious. Why do I need music that makes it worse?' But ugliness, which tells us far more about ourselves than beauty does, suggests total candor. It may even bring us one step closer to redemption. The Fall's music is harrowing because it's trying to push ugliness to its breaking point and come out on the other side. It refuses to comfort you because the work is hard and going there requires feeling real dread. But the breakthrough, however fleeting, is exultant.

Pitchfork saw the album as the apogee of The Fall's ever-present tightrope walk between instinct and skill, a walk the group was, almost unbelievably, still able to manage at the time of Mark's death:

> But what does it sound like, you may ask? Well, it sounds like The Fall. It sounds like a group of five talented musicians trying to play as brilliantly stupid as possible, while a sixth fellow from the docks hops on stage, grabs the mike, and fights his way through the morass scorched-earth style. It sounds like the primordial ooze that birthed touchstones like The Stooges and the Velvet Underground come to life, nursing a bitch of a hangover and a vendetta. It's something you're born with, not something you learn. And, as on most Fall records, but especially this one, it's something to behold.

Discussing the 2005 reissue of the album in *The Observer*, Kitty Empire was equally convinced that *Hex's* main strength was that it got the 'brilliantly stupid' balance bang on:[141]

> Fall fans can argue long and loudly about which is The Fall's finest album. For many people's money, though, it could well be *Hex Enduction Hour* ... From its sublime title on in, the elements that made The Fall unique coalesced particularly auspiciously on *Hex*. Mark E. Smith's band had moved on from their scrappy, atonal beginnings into a loose, flowing form of their own. Guitarist and Smith's

[141] Which Steve described earlier as 'don't make mistakes but don't get too professional'.

wife-to-be Brix had yet to beam her strange California sunshine into the Mancunian murk. Smith's vitriol is by turns gnomic, tetchy and funny, especially about music critics on 'Hip Priest'. The long-suffering Craig Scanlon and Marc Riley (subsequently a successful radio presenter) accompany him with shards of guitar riffs and a surprising amount of rhythm: opener 'The Classical' even points ahead half a decade to the Happy Mondays.

John Doran: *Hex* is the received, canonical, super-massive-black-hole at the centre of The Fall galaxy. Even *Record Collector* knows what a big deal *Hex Enduction Hour* is.

Not that we should necessarily care, and Mark certainly didn't, but *Hex* has also been cited by other musicians on occasion. Stephen Malkmus and Pavement's fascination with *Hex* has been frequently mentioned. *Slanted and Enchanted*'s cover owes a large debt to the sleeve, and the song 'Our Singer' bears more than a passing resemblance to 'Hip Priest' (Malkmus later admitted they were 'related'). Pavement also recorded a fairly unconvincing cover version of 'The Classical' for John Peel in 1997.

Asked in 1999 by Everett True about her obsession with Stevie Nicks, Courtney Love was moved to reply:

Courtney Love: What Stevie Nicks obsession? 'Go Your Own Way' is one of the best white pop songs ever written, absolutely. There are songs on *Rumours* that are genius, but there's as much *Hex Enduction Hour* as Stevie Nicks stuff on *Celebrity Skin*.

Moreover Kurt Cobain, Suede, Franz Ferdinand, LCD Soundsystem and others have all mentioned *Hex Enduction Hour* as well. But even when they're ripping off Fall songs, none of the bands that cite The Fall really sound anything like *Hex*, or The Fall, at all. Although it looks like it should be, it isn't particularly easy to make a record like *Hex Enduction Hour*. Perhaps the most important thing to remember is that the group didn't really know what they were doing, and it's a lot easier to be authentic when you're playing in the only style you can master.

All of which is why the period when *Hex Enduction Hour* was created is a good place to start if you want to know how the group worked. But do people cite *Hex Enduction Hour* because it does what The Fall is supposed to do, or is our idea of what The Fall should sound like based on *Hex Enduction Hour*'s template? That's the dilemma we face when examining every band's so-called seminal LPs of course, but then most bands don't release thirty-odd albums by umpteen different line-ups. It's entirely possible that the majority of members of The Fall haven't even heard *Hex Enduction Hour* all the way through – it was certainly the case that Mark discouraged newer recruits from checking out the group's back catalogue. And later iterations of The Fall had proper musicians – Simon Rogers, Steve Trafford, Tim Presley and more, as well as the group's final line-up – who could play anything and any way they wanted, but Mark still managed to make them sound like The Fall. If our idea of what constitutes that Fall sound is informed by *Hex Enduction Hour*, as created by non-musicians, how is that possible? While the easy answer is to say that it was all down to Mark anyway, a cursory glance at the songwriting credits on all those albums shows that's not entirely the case, especially given the fact that Mark was never overly troubled by the need to give credit where credit's due. We know The Fall would never have worked as Mark E. Smith and some session musicians, they were always a group, and every member brought something different to the table. But they always sounded like The Fall, and The Fall sound like *Hex Enduction Hour*. How? Have a bleedin' guess.

Mark E. Smith: The thing about browsing through these books is that you don't find out anything about me at all, do you?

NOT FIT FOR: HEX END

Index of Quotes

One way or the other, I've tried to give the original source for all the quotes in the book. If the source is quoted in the main text, then obviously it isn't given here. N.B: You'll notice that although I managed to speak to most of the main players involved in *Hex*'s creation, sadly there are no quotes from Karl. I did my best to track him down, including a speculative trip to his old house in Rawtenstall with Steve, but it wasn't to be. I hope I haven't done him a disservice. He was, without a doubt, one of the best drummers I've ever heard, and it was an absolute honour, if sometimes a white-knuckle ride, to have been in a two-drummer line-up with him.

'I'm still very proud of that album...' Mark E. Smith *Renegade: The Lives and Tales of Mark E. Smith*. This often-hilarious tome was ghost written by Austin Collings, who Mark began throwing under the bus almost from the minute it was finished. I reckon it's a pretty accurate document of Mark's own words, despite what he later made out. That said, Collings's habitual rendering of Mark saying 'fellah' as 'fellow' never fails to jar. I know the former began as a different pronunciation of the latter, but they're not the same word anymore, are they? Unless otherwise stated, *Renegade* is the source of Mark's quotes herein.

'There's always some cunt...' Mark quoted in Q, July 2015.

'Even if it's a fool's errand...' is from John Doran's review of the Sanctuary *Hex* reissue in the December 2009 issue of *Record Collector*.

'I always try and put a little crack in it...' Mark quoted in *Tape Delay: Confessions from the Eighties Underground* by Charles Neal. 'Lyrics change shape...' is from Mick Middles's book *The Fall*. 'And do you know...' is from 'Becks Induction Hour: Mark E. Smith On The LP That Nearly Ended The Fall' – a 2018 *The Quietus* article based on an interview with Mark by John Doran in 2007.

'When I started buying records...' is also Mark quoted in Mick Middles's *The Fall*, written with complete cooperation from Mark (he gets a co-author credit), but which nonetheless he also later repudiated. Mark's relationship with Mick, whom he'd known for years, never recovered, unsurprisingly. From 'this culture...' onwards it's Mark in *The Independent*, 28th May 2004.

'What if he wasn't a genius...' Paul Morley, quoted in *The Fall: The Wonderful and Frightening World of Mark E. Smith,* a 2005 BBC4 documentary. It's a good, if unkind, quote, and no doubt it's crossed all our minds briefly, but Morley didn't really believe it, or he'd never have appeared in the film, surely?

'Compared to The Fall, even Dylan's...' from Stewart Lee's 'A Primer to The Fall' (www.stewartlee.co.uk)

'His superb drumming...' from Graham Lock's *NME* review of *Live at the Witch Trials* 24th March 1979.

'Karl Burns ... is not...'; 'a cross between...' From Allan Jones incredibly bitchy *Melody Maker* review of *Live at the Witch Trials,* 24th March 1979.

'It was becoming hard work...' Martin quoted in an interview with *Pop Matters:* 'Motorways, Bank Robbers, and Other Delights: A Conversation with Martin Bramah of Blue Orchids' by Jedd Beaudoin. (See www.popmatters.com).

'The energy a line-up change...' Mark quoted in Tony Fletcher's *Jamming!* fanzine. A good number of these old interviews can be found online.

'Like you get all these Scottish bands...' Mark in conversation with *Distant Violins,* an Australian fanzine that stretched the interview over three issues (not that they were starved of interviewees or anything) from August 1982 to March 1983.

'At fifteen dear old Gong...' The marvellous Mr Grant Showbiz, interviewed by Martin Peters for *The Pseud Mag,* a Fall fanzine set up by Dave Bromwich (aka 'Fall Fan Dave') which ran from December 2004 until 2007, and featured interviews with several of The Fall's key players (and me).

'I'd seen Alternative TV...' Personal communication with Grant. One of the joys of writing this book is that it afforded me the opportunity to discuss the group and the album with others who shared the experience, like Mr Showbiz here. I've known him nearly forty years. We *never* talked about this stuff. All Grant's quotes are from our discussions, unless stated otherwise.

'I was always proud...' John Brierley on Facebook.

'The sound on *Dragnet* either freaked people out...' Most quotes from Marc and Steve are from a lovely, rambling conversation/interview conducted on 2nd April 2019. We'd just seen Manchester United beaten 2-1 by Wolves as part of a particularly dismal run of form. Manchester City were running rampant and with Marc being a massive Blue it was important that we had something else to talk about.

'If it's me and yer granny on bongos...' The misquoted version is, ironically, probably Mark's most famous utterance. The original source was a particularly grumpy *NME* interview in February 1998 by John Robinson. It's nestled amongst several other openly contemptuous comments about the group, which gives a good indication of the dire state of inter-band relations ahead of the American tour scheduled for the following month. As you probably know, the tour was an unmitigated disaster and lead to the final departure of two of The Fall's most significant members.

'[Mark] asked me if...' All quotes from Geoff Travis are from *Document and Eyewitness: An Intimate History of Rough Trade* by Neil Taylor. As I noted in *Leave The Capital*, I don't think I ever had a one-to-one conversation with Geoff.

'The form of "The N.W.R.A." is as alien...' and 'plays like some improbable mulching...' Mark Fisher: 'Memorex for the Krakens' in *Mark E. Smith and The Fall: Art, Music and Politics*. This book, edited by Michael Goddard and Ben Halligan, began as a symposium on Mark's work at The University of Salford in 2008. There are a number of quotes from the book included here. As you'd expect, it's a pretty cerebral tome. It's well worth checking out, but it's not cheap, and I wouldn't recommend tackling it after a more than a couple of pints. It's also worth bearing in mind that Mark wasn't massively impressed by the symposium and sent his sister Caroline down to disrupt proceedings. He later said, 'I feel sorry for the people who went to that symposium. People who'd come from Austria, saved up, just to see some windbag who's probably one of my old enemies and is a lecturer now, getting six hundred nicker a week to buy next month's Bordeaux.'

'*Slates* was pretty much my album...' Grant in *The Pseud Mag* fanzine. He followed up this quote with 'Mark, Geoff or Adrian; if I've got that wrong forgive me!!!!' But as the next quote confirms, he was bang on.

'I ended up helping Grant' from an interview with Adrian Sherwood for *Test Pressing* online magazine: www.testpressing.org

'What I'm going for is a well-produced noise...' Mark from an interview with Radio 1's Richard

Skinner, quoted in Simon Ford's *Hip Priest: The Story of Mark E. Smith and The Fall*. The book is one of the better places to go for factual info about Mark and the group. Ford does blot his copybook a little by taking a spoof interview in *The Biggest Library Yet* (another defunct Fall print fanzine) with *Emmerdale*'s Lisa Riley at face value. The fake interview presents her as Marc's sister. She isn't, of course, and since Steve got into trouble with Marc's *real* sister for not mentioning her by name in *The Big Midweek* – Hello Tina.

'I was a big fan...' like all quotes from Colin Irwin (unless taken from the original *Melody Maker* article) this is from a personal conversation with Colin, who I hadn't spoken to since we landed back in London following the Iceland tour. He's finally thawed out, if you're wondering.

'I realised that if I parked...' Einar Örn from 'Björk, KUKL and Purrkur Pillnikk – the anarcho-punk roots of Iceland's music scene', a 2015 *Guardian* article by Dave Simpson.

'One of my finer and lovelier experiences...' Kay Carroll, or Kay Bateman as she is now. Another personal communication. How far we've all come. N.B. I've referred to Kay as 'Carroll' throughout to avoid confusion.

'We had half of Iceland...' From personal conversations with Craig.

He's rarely given interviews since leaving The Fall, so I'm particularly grateful he agreed to speak to me about the album. His perspective on things is absent from most previous attempts to tell the story of The Fall and is sorely missed.

'It was so bleak there...' Marc speaking to John Doran in 2013 for an article in *The Quietus* 'Jeepers Creepers: Marc Riley's Favourite Albums', published 25th February 2013.

'Iceland was a closed...' is from 'Becks Induction Hour'. In *The Quietus* article a quarter of the population turned up, by the time *Renegade* came out two years later it was a third. In *The Quietus* he also helpfully points out that the audience included 'Women, children, the lot'.

'I wrote "Hip Priest"...' For the record, in *Renegade*, Mark also claims to have written 'every note' of 'Totally Wired', 'the guitar bits and the riffs' to 'Touch Sensitive' etc etc.

'It was a bit of a joke...' Mark, from the aforementioned interview with Richard Skinner, this time transcribed by The Annotated Fall (see below).

Danny Baker as the 'Dan' of the song is a theory expounded on The Annotated Fall website – www.annotatedfall.doomby.com – which is well worth a trip round, with the slight caveat that because it's collaborative, all theories are given equal weight.

'I'm not a private person...' Mark in 'Becks Induction Hour' again.

'That gets a bit personal...' from an unpublished interview with Mark E. Smith in 1981 by J. Neo Marvin. The full fascinating discussion was eventually made available here: http://jneomarvin.com/interviews-of-our-times/the-fall-unpublished-1981/

'There may have been...' Jonathan Demme quoted on the promo CD for the US release of The Infotainment Scan.

'It's odd with stuff...' is from 'Becks Induction Hour'. 'I could have a mansion by now...' is from Renegade.

'The boys in the band...' is from Robin Purves's essay '"Humbled in Iceland": On Improvisation during The Fall' in Mark E. Smith and The Fall: Art, Music and Politics.

'He said he wanted...' is from the aforementioned 'Jeepers Creepers' feature in The Quietus.

'I like to make sure they know...' Mark speaking to Sean O'Hagan in the Guardian, 16th Jan 2005. As this is the first thing I've written since I got my degree from the OU, I was particularly pleased with this quote from later in the article: 'I'm plagued with graduates reading things into the songs. There's a glut of graduates in the world.'

'James Brown was as ferociously professional...' is also from an essay in Mark E. Smith and The Fall: Art, Music and Politics, this time by Angus McDonald: '"The Sound of The Fall, the Truth of this Movement of Error": A True Companion, an Ambivalent Friendship, an Ethic of Truths'. Snappy title!

'I went into it thinking...' the first half of the quote is from 'Becks Induction Hour', the second half is from Renegade.

'I persuaded Mark E. Smith...' Steve Jameson quoted in Document and Eyewitness: An Intimate History of Rough Trade.

'They didn't like the sentiment...' is from Renegade. 'We stuck with 'em as long as we could...' is from the 1982 Distant Violins interview. 'Slates was the final...' is again from Renegade, 27 years after the Distant Violins interview. He didn't mellow towards Rough Trade over the years, did he? 'It was none of their business, so I walked' is from Q, March 1994.

'They were always alright...' Distant Violins interview 1982.

'Prior to starting Kamera...' Chris Youle's quotes are from personal communications. The first time he's given his side of the story, I think.

'Bonaparte was mail-order...' I had a tremendous conversation with Saul Galpern while researching the book. His story of how he nearly signed Mark and The Fall to Nude in the late nineties, which involves one or possibly two other Manchester music legends, is brilliant.

'That's the Fall...' Martin Bramah, from an interview with the *Fred Negro* online magazine www.frednegro.com.au

'As you can see...' Mark onstage at Xtreems in Brighton on 21st October 1981.

'I was the singer...' and subsequent quotes from Richard Mazda, are from interviews conducted for this book. Richard is now an actor and runs a theatre group in New York. Not one for standing still.

'A lot of those kids...' Mark speaking to Barney Hoskyns in the *NME*, 14th November 1981

'That song actually...' Mark in the *NME* again, this time talking to Don Watson, 1st October 1983. Note that in the space of two years the 'young healthy kids' who 'went to The Wigan Casino' and thought of The Fall as 'the same as all these other pretentious groups' have grown into 'old soul boys who like The Fall'.

'We had two drummers, and studios...' from *The Quietus* 'Becks Induction Hour' article again. All credit to John Doran, Mark really opened up in this interview.

'That's the good thing about *Hex*...' the quote is from *Renegade*, albeit in a slightly different order.

'The problem for "normal" ears...' Stuart Estell – the quote's from a discussion about 'The Classical' on the Fall online forum.

'There's no definitive Fall song...' Nathanial Friedman for *Billboard*, 26th January 2018.

'The dissonance achieved...' Richard Witts, quoted in *Mark E. Smith and The Fall: Art, Music and Politics*. Now a lecturer on music at Edinburgh University.

'It was a hopeless task...' Simon Rogers speaking to Martin Peters in *The Pseud Mag,* 2006.

'He was the host of *The South Bank Show*...' John Doran, discussing the album as part of Cultish Events' series 'Alt-Classic Album Playback'. A video of the talk is available on YouTube.

'And did you see...' interview with *Sounds*, 8th May 1982. It's increasingly prevalent to dig up dubious comments from a long time ago, and it's often unfair to do so, which I accept it may well be here. But I think it's useful in this case to highlight the context of the time in which Mark was speaking, and to point out that Mark's rejection of any suggestion of racism is taken at absolutely face value by the *Sounds* journalist.

'His ability to combine first, second and third character narratives…' is from an online discussion/review: 'The Fall - Album by Album', hosted by Steve Hoffman: https://forums.stevehoffman.tv

'Plagiarisation and blackboard type people…' is from the press release for The Fall's tour of the US in June/July 1981.

'It was 1982 and Motown's…' The rather touching *We Are Cult* obituary by Jon Wilde, which included the Motown story, is available here: www.wearecult.rocks/mark-e-smith

'The funny thing was this guy at Motown…' is from an interview Mark did with our old friend Colin Irwin, *Melody Maker*, 20th October 1984.

'It was all signed…' is from *Q*, April 1994: 'I Didn't Get Where I Am Today' by David Cavanagh.

'I don't wish to be pedantic' is from Mick Middle's book *The Fall*.

'Motown were opening up…' personal conversation with the splendid Mr Richard Thomas, who acted as The Fall's manager during the transition from Rough Trade to Beggars Banquet. His memory for dates and events around that time is astonishing.

You can see him playing 'Pat McHat' in the video for 'Kicker Conspiracy'.

'"And This Day", the thing that finishes off the LP…' Richard Skinner interview 1982.

'Who is the king shag corpse…' Is from an essay about cult musicians by Bob Stanley in the *Guardian*, 22nd August 2008.

'What about Norman Mailer…' is taken from 'Life lessons: Mark E. Smith on bullying, the occult and why Stalin had the right idea', an interview with Robert Chalmers published in *The Independent*, 13th November 2011.

'The taped effects…' is from Robert Walker's '"Dictaphonics": Acoustics and Primitive Recording in the Music of The Fall', in *Mark E. Smith and The Fall: Art, Music and Politics* again. He's referring to the song 'Music Scene', but it's even more applicable here.

'When The Fall put two or more disparate…' is also from Walker's '"Dictaphonics": Acoustics and Primitive Recording in the Music of The Fall'.

'"I'm Into C.B." seemed impossibly annoying…' is taken from an article Stewart Lee wrote for *Going for a Song*, as reproduced on Stewart's website.

'I never imagined it to be like this…' is from *The Big Midweek*, by Steve Hanley and Olivia Piekarski. I must read it.

'I first met Karl Burns on the street...' is from an interview with Martin called 'Primal Scenes' by Simon Ford, printed in *The Wire* May 2002.

'I like the cover...' is from the *Sounds* interview with Sandy Robertson in May 1982.

'I'd never seen anything like it...' is from a brilliant interview in *The Quietus* by Luke Turner: 'Mark E. Smith Of The Fall On Art & The Artist'. That's also the source of Mark's quote about the symposium which lead to the book *Mark E. Smith and The Fall: Art, Music and Politics*. Given how many quotes from that book it contains, he'd have hated *this*, wouldn't he?

'Whenever I say anything...'; 'Smith's polemic continues...' and 'I was talking to one woman' are from an interview Mark did in 1992 with *Frieze* magazine. The article was by written Michael Bracewell and Jon Wilde.

'The main thing is that both...' is from a personal communication from Dr. Michael Nath. Blimey, get me.

'A sense of tension exists...' is from Paul Wilson's 'Language Scraps: Mark E. Smith's Handwriting and the Typography of The Fall', in *Mark E. Smith and The Fall: Art, Music and Politics*.

'Einar took us way out...' is from an article about The Fall's most important albums in *Uncut* by Dave Simpson, July 2019.

'I'm dead proud of that record...' is from *NME* 15th January 1983 interview by Richard Cook; 'I don't think there is anything...' is from Mick Middles *The Fall*; 'and I wanted to try and capture a rawness...' interview with Jack Barron, *Sounds*, 13th August 1983; 'I thought we were getting a bit restricted...' *Masterbag* interview by Helen Fitzgerald, 1982.

'We had to leave Kamera...' is from David Cavanagh's article in *Q*, April 1994. From 'meant that we had to...' onwards it's *Renegade*.

'A repetitive, pulverising barrage of unpleasantness...' *Q* April 2019, which contained Stewart Lee's essay on *Hex*.

'Fall fans can argue...' *The Observer*, 9th January 2005.

'What Stevie Nicks obsession...?' Courtney Love's interview with Everett True was in the Seattle newspaper *The Stranger*, 25th February 1999.

'The thing about browsing through these books...' Mark in *The Independent*, 28th May 2004.

Thanks...

To everyone who was kind enough to speak to me for this book, either in person, by phone or by email, thank you for your time and patience. Thanks also to the many brilliant writers whose work I have pored over while putting this together and consequently quoted liberally herein. Special mention should also go to The Annotated Fall, Reformation Post TPM and thefall.org websites, and The Mighty Fall Facebook page for the incredible work they do keeping interest in The Fall alive (and special thanks to Barrie for his input on The Fall's stage gear). Huge thanks to the marvellous Mr Stewart Lee, both for his wonderful foreword and for showing me just what you can do with a well-placed footnote. Thanks also to Dr. Michael Nath, lecturer, novelist and Wyndham Lewis expert, who was gracious enough to correct my naive assumptions on Vorticism and provide some brilliant quotes. I also need to thank Ian and Isabel at Route for suggesting this project and for their support and encouragement.

Thanks to Julie, Roseanna, Adam and Nathan, for the finest times of my life.

Belated thanks also to my sister-in-law Lynn, not least for the Neil Sedaka story that didn't make it into *Leave The Capital*. Buy me a pint and I'll tell you.

Massive thanks, of course, to Craig, Karl, Marc, Steve, Kay, Grant and Richard, without whose sterling efforts you would now be holding a blank notebook.

Finally, thank you to the irreplaceable Mark E. Smith. A unique, and uniquely talented, individual, I think we can all agree.

Paul Hanley was the drummer in The Fall from 1980–85 and now plays with Brix & The Extricated. His debut book *Leave The Capital: A History of Manchester Music in 13 Recordings* was nominated for the ARSC Award for Excellence in Historical Recorded Sound Research.

For more on this book, and Route's full book list, visit:
www.route-online.com